ARE YOUNG CHILDREN EGOCENTRIC?

155.413 ARE
COX

22 APR 2025   **WITHDRAWN**

Are Young Children Egocentric?

EDITED BY M. V. COX

Batsford Academic and Educational Ltd

First published 1980

© Maureen Cox 1980

Batsford Academic and Educational Ltd
4 Fitzhardinge Street, London W1H 0AH

ISBN 0 7134 37200

Typeset by Computacomp (UK) Ltd, Fort William, Scotland

Printed in Great Britain by
Billing & Son Ltd
London, Guildford and Worcester

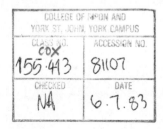

British Library Cataloguing in Publication Data

Are young children egocentric? (*Conference*), *York, 1978*
   Are young children egocentric?
   1. Egoism in children – Congresses
   I. British Psychological Society.
   Annual Conference, York, 1978
   II. Cox, M V
   155.4'13   BF723.E/

ISBN 0–7134–3720–0

Contents

Contributors

GAVIN BREMNER
Department of Psychology, University of Lancaster

GEORGE BUTTERWORTH
Department of Psychology, University of Southampton

M. V. COX
Department of Psychology, University of York

NORMAN FREEMAN
Department of Psychology, University of Bristol

PAUL LIGHT
Department of Psychology, University of Southampton

E. J. ROBINSON and W. P. ROBINSON
School of Education, University of Bristol

Preface

Although Jean Piaget started working on his theory of cognitive development early in this century, it was not until the late 1950s and 1960s that its impact was felt to any great extent in English-speaking countries. Since educational practice is closely linked to theories of cognitive development it is naturally in the field of education that Piaget's theory has been particularly influential. Indeed, it often appears that the theory has been accepted wholesale as a proven state of affairs rather than as a set of hypotheses which need to be tested. I think it is true to say that although the theory has also been important in psychology – it has presented a challenge to existing theories and has provided tremendous impetus for research and thought on the nature of development – it has been treated with somewhat more scepticism.

The notion of egocentrism itself was introduced quite early in Piaget's first book *The Language and Thought of the Child*, 1926. He considers that this pervading characteristic of the young child's thought is due to his inability to decentre, i.e. to differentiate between subject and object, and therefore he remains unaware that his own experiences of the world and those of others may differ. Piaget's writings, however, are difficult to follow and it often *appears* that he says some contradictory things. A major purpose in compiling this book is to clarify the meaning of egocentrism. I have been dismayed to find that the notion of egocentrism, along with Piaget's whole theory, is often accepted unquestioningly as a fundamental feature of young children's thought processes. It sometimes appears that it has attained this status by 'squatters' rights'. Another aim of the book, therefore, is to provide a critical appraisal of the concept in the light of research evidence.

The original idea for this book came from the symposium of the same title which was organized on behalf of the Developmental Psychology Section of the British Psychological Society for the BPS Annual Conference at York in 1978. The symposium was chaired by George Butterworth and included papers by Gavin Bremner, Paul Light, Elizabeth and Peter Robinson, and myself; Norman Freeman led a discussion following the presentation of papers. I am very grateful to Norman for suggesting that I convene the symposium and, subsequently, edit this book.

7

In organizing the layout of the book, I have generally followed the plan of the symposium. Norman Freeman introduces the topic of egocentrism and shows how each author's particular subject-area fits into it, and George Butterworth discusses some of the issues raised by the topic. Both these chapters provide the background for later ones in which authors examine the concept of egocentrism within their own research area.

The critical stance which the contributors have taken towards the concept of egocentrism will be of relevance to all those concerned with cognitive development. In particular, those involved in teaching will need to consider carefully these criticisms of a way of thinking about young children which has become deeply ingrained. Such an attitude has resulted in considerable underestimation of children's capabilities. I hope that an informed view of the issues involved will lead to a more positive and optimistic approach to education.

M. V. Cox

1

Introduction of the diverse work that the concept of egocentrism has inspired

NORMAN FREEMAN

Jean Piaget has often been praised for his 'clinical observations'. These are extracts from conversations with the children undergoing his experiments, and they bring many of his books to life. In a paper written in 1968 he lays stress on how his theory of child development is a dynamic one, involving many interacting processes. His clinical observation of individual children's puzzlement and discovery gives intuitive support to some such view against the sterility of the old-fashioned 'association-of-ideas' approach. There is every reason, therefore, to begin with a clinical observation upon my elder daughter.

SARAH	five years four months, (looking down at her legs). 'So that's how knees go. They are just roundy. I never knew that. I shall always draw them in my drawings from now on.'
N.H.F.	'You do want to draw knees then?'
SARAH	'Oh yes, course I do.'
N.H.F.	'Why? Your drawings are fine anyway.'
SARAH	'I know, but it would get them more realisticker.'
N.H.F.	'O.K. Can you do it?'
SARAH	'Oh yes, just roundy.'

Her claim is that she understood both about having knees and the value of showing them in her drawings for meeting realistic criteria, but that she had lacked the link which would bring both understandings together for public consumption. If we did not know about that missing link of 'how they go', it would be easy to underestimate both her stored knowledge and her criterial knowledge. Children can have good understanding of both types, but lack knowledge of how to put their understanding to work. Much of what you are going to read in this book illuminates the problems children face in implementing their understanding.

Here is an example from the chapter by Elizabeth and Peter Robinson. They take up the question of whether it can be right to say that young children are egocentric on the grounds that they seem to assume that their own speech is perfectly comprehensible and therefore that the listener is at fault if something goes wrong in the communication. They report some beautifully original analytic work and towards the end they suggest: 'If the speech can be shown to have ...

(symptoms of apparent egocentrism) ... only because no one has made it clear to the children what needs to be done in a situation to improve communicative efficiency and that such instruction quickly changes their behaviour, then the label "egocentrism" can be dropped.' If that suggestion holds good under the scrutiny of future researchers, then the term 'egocentrism' will have played an immensely useful role: it is a beautiful death for a concept if it can inspire researchers to investigate children's understanding in such a way that the transition can be made to working *with* children.

At the moment, work is still largely in the first phase, and it would be grossly mistaken to herald the end of the working life of the concept, eagerly though every scientist looks forward to developing a theory to a new stage which surpasses the old. Let us stay for the moment with the study of communication to draw some important lessons. One comes from Piaget (1928). He suggest on p. 207 that children have a 'habit' of 'always believing themselves to be understood': that 'they are permanently under the impression that they understand each other and have no suspicion of the egocentric character of their thought'. So the speaker indulges naturally in 'faulty expression' in which 'the very language is egocentric', and the listener 'does not listen because he thinks all along that he can understand everything, and because he assimilates everything he hears to his own point of view' (p. 208). In short, both participants in childish conversation are egocentric: the speaker does not accommodate to the listener's needs, and the listener simply assimilates the message to his own egocentric viewpoint. This is the situation which the Robinsons examine, with some quite surprising results. Notice what Piaget is describing: two ways in which egocentrism can be restrictive because two children have been given different jobs to do by the experimenter. They are both 'negative signs' of egocentrism. But Piaget (1970) also stresses that when a single child is studied, the relationships between accommodating to the outside world and assimilating it can have both positive and negative aspects, which are 'inseparable'. Rotman (1978) sums up this difficult idea very clearly in his sixth chapter where he talks of Piaget's view of accommodation and assimilation as being 'two opposing biological tendencies: the principle of external adaptation or "opening" whereby the organism extends its response to, and ultimately its measure of control over, even larger environments, and internal adaptation or "integration" under which it grows more complex and independent of its environment ...' These are both positive processes, essential to establish in working order and 'equilibrium'. Could it be that the negative side of childish communication is that the speaker is under the delusion that he has effective control before the conversation even starts so need make no extra effort to have his wishes obeyed; and the listener is under the converse delusion that he too need exert no extra effort to be in control of the environment so that what he does must necessarily adequately fulfil the wishes of the speaker? The image that comes to mind then is of a *confrontation* between two blindfolded people each of whom thinks that he is necessarily right in what he does, rather than a *conversation* in which each assimilates the message of the other and accommodates to the other. Clearly, it needs detailed research to disentangle whether the children are really under the delusion, or whether they are not but lack the fine control skills to stage-manage a meeting of minds.

Piaget (1928) ends up by backing a version of the 'delusion account'. He is very pessimistic about children's social skills: 'The social instinct is late in developing. The first critical stage occurs at the age seven to eight ...' (p. 209). Can this be true? It is obviously false in the sense that children have been exposed to a great deal of *social experience* right from birth and have had to live with that. Paul Light's chapter in this book takes up the issue of how adept young children may be at role-taking, which inevitably means freeing themselves from their own viewpoint to some extent. As he observes, 'if we say of an adult that he is "being egocentric" we do not usually mean that he is cognitively deficient and incapable of the inferences involved in taking another's perspective. Rather we mean that he does not feel the necessity to accommodate to the other's viewpoint, or that he is *insensitive* to it.' His conclusion, arrived at by work quite independent of the Robinsons', converges beautifully with theirs: 'If a distinction is made between competence and performance, then our emphasis is on the latter'.

Light's work contains another strand to it, interwoven with the social one. If we talk about someone being able, ready or willing to 'take another person's point of view' is this not a metaphor drawn from experience with spatial relations? Accordingly he comments on children's abilities to guess what another person can see, and their abilities to show something to someone else who cannot see it from their particular position. In fact, this 'spatial egocentrism problem' bulks very large in Piaget's argument, and it has often been claimed that children's problems in shifting viewpoint provide conclusive evidence upon the egocentric nature of children up to the age of seven or eight years. The classic task is to sit a child down in front of an array of objects, then to sit down oneself on the other side of the table, and to ask the child to choose the photograph which would show what you can see not what he himself can see. It is very impressive when the child chooses his own view. But does this mean that Piaget is right in suggesting that the child believes that the adult has to share the child's own view rather than having a different one of his own? Maureen Cox's chapter lays out a great deal of evidence on this. She shows that indeed children will very often behave in an apparently grossly egocentric manner, yet they can have very sophisticated understanding of spatial relations: '... the young child does expect his own view to change when he moves to a new position'. However, that in itself will not tell us the extent of his 'knowledge of other person's views'. Perhaps we have here a problem which is just like the one which the case-study at the start of this Introduction served to raise: the child might know what his view is, know that the other observer's different viewpoint entails a different view, but not quite know what to do about it. There is some evidence which supports that notion. Even adults tend to give 'egocentric' responses in complicated viewpoint-shift tasks. What sort of odd 'insensitivity' is this, and can it be the same as that so easily demonstrable in young children? Cox ends by saying that Piaget was right when he observed that young children find it very difficult to predict another person's view accurately, but that this does not entail 'egocentrism'. Freeman (1980) provides supportive evidence.

What the three chapters just mentioned (by Cox, Light and the Robinsons), diverse though they be, all have in common are two strands: an analysis of the relationships between knowing what has to be done and how to do it, and the relations between social and spatial responsiveness: (a) either getting someone to understand something new or showing that you understand something new, and (b) getting someone to see something new or showing that you understand about seeing something new. There are two more chapters which place almost their entire emphasis on the spatial relations problem. My own chapter on drawing takes up the repeated assertion by Piaget and Inhelder (1948) that spatial egocentrism can be seen as clearly in children's relatively free drawings as in their behaviour in imposed tasks. The symptoms of egocentrism all manifest themselves in a relative insensitivity to the structure of the scene which the child is attempting to portray: a defect in 'realism'. Piaget and Inhelder (1969) assert that young children are overwhelmingly infantile realists: why then should they so often be bad at it, and why should they so often churn out a stereotyped drawing even when the scene changes dramatically in front of their eyes? What I hope the experimental evidence I cite serves to show is that they are much more scene-sensitive than adult contemplators of their drawings have realized up to now (evidence which can only support the arguments of Cox and Light), and that there is a hidden orderliness to their drawings even when they seem to be grossly unrealistic. The rules that children operate when constructing drawings are often very different from those operated by adults, and fill the gap between knowing what has to be done and knowing how to do it. Some of these rules are quite invisible to adults; they only become manifest when one establishes a primitive type of social relationship with the child by playing drawing-completion games. The child's understanding of spatial relations only becomes clear if one alters his social relations, and converts drawing from a solitary hole-and-corner pursuit to a shared game. And of course, yet again, adults show some symptoms of apparent egocentrism in their drawings. ...

Finally, if young children do indeed share far more of 'our world' than Piaget gave them credit for, how about babies, who surely have to be 'inducted' into accurate knowledge of social and spatial relations? Egocentrism in the first year of life is a cornerstone of Piaget's work. Gavin Bremner's chapter examines the matter in great detail. A very striking aspect of his work is to take very simple marks of spatial egocentrism in babies and show how complicated a theory of their behaviour has to be. It is always refreshing when this is done. Here is a key example. A baby of some nine or ten months of age is seated in a highchair. On a table in front of him are two sunken wells, each covered with a cloth. You show the baby an extremely desirable object (a bunch of keys, say) and hide it in one of the wells. You wait three seconds, then push the table up to the highchair and encourage the baby to get the object. Then, gently but firmly, the object is taken away from the baby and the exercise repeated. On the fourth trial you conspicuously hide the object in the other well. Very often, the baby will go straight for the *first* well (and then, often, stop dead in puzzlement). Why this inflexibility in search, this lack of freedom to alter the initial spatial relation between self and place of search? Does this reflect a thinking which is 'in a sense, still magical' (Bower, 1977, p. 118)? Bremner's work analyses this curious error in detail. Apparently the baby has not taken a decisive step towards freeing himself from the *context* of initial successful finding towards freedom of action across spatial relationships, towards a breaking of this initial 'action-environment link'. Yet Bremner shows that if the baby's spatial experience is taken into account in designing the experiments, the baby comes out as less egocentric than supposed. The suggestion at the end of the chapter is that the baby has a greater understanding of spatial relations that Piaget gives credit for, but that there are many experiences which the baby undergoes which activate coping strategies for locating objects which give the appearance of great inflexibility. The baby needs cues to tell him not to rely too much on these primitive strategies. When may such cues be picked up by the baby? Perhaps when he starts to crawl around under his own steam, often around the same age of nine or so months. Again the emphasis is put upon the learning of performance strategies rather than upon deep cognitive limitations. And again, as Bremner points out, adults too appear to behave egocentrically in special cases. So, yet again, one wants to distinguish between the rational use of a self-referent code for certain purposes by adults and a theory which says that the infantile mentality is necessarily self-centred.

Now this Introduction may be ended. There are two threads running through the work of the authors. First, the way in which one gains access to the child mind involves delicate decisions as to when a particular action is a symptom of the child not knowing what to do, when it testifies rather to him not knowing how to do it, and whether the child has the same aims as the adult. This is traced through his apparent comprehension of social relations and spatial relations: taking a new view of things. The second thread is the relationship between an explanation of the behaviour-patterns of the child and an imaginative reconstruction of the child's experiences. The emphasis is primarily on the former. There are many, many books in which adult authors try heroically to 'put themselves in the child's place'. Is this not liable to be rather egocentric of the adults? The work laid out here is analytic work, showing the way in which new research has shown new things that we have to explain, so that we can lay the structure of our action alongside that of the young child for cross-comparison. As a result, theory will have to be quite complicated, and discriminations will have to be rather fine. It is very challenging.

By now there will be many readers who are impatient with this Introduction. What is it about this concept of egocentrism which seems to enable it to take so many guises across such a vast area of psychology? It is, I agree, high time to explain and define the concept. Here I hand over to George Butterworth. He was one of the first people in this country to study the concept in its first line of defence: infancy. His analysis leads straight on to Bremner's chapter, thence onwards to older children, then to social relations. Whether Piaget comes out well or badly at the end I leave it to the reader to judge. In the long run it does not matter. What does matter is whether one can have a reasonable understanding of child development without the type of research reported here. To us, it seems unlikely.

References

BOWER, T. G. R. (1977) *A Primer of Infant Development*. London: Freeman.

FREEMAN, N. H. (1980) *Strategies of Representation in Young Children. Analysis of Spatial Skills and Drawing Processes*. London: Academic Press.

PIAGET, J. (1928) *Judgement and Reasoning in the Child*. London: Routledge and Kegan Paul.

PIAGET, J. (1968) 'Le point de vue de Piaget'. *Journal International de Psychologie*, 3, 281–299.

PIAGET, J. (1970) 'Introduction to LAURENDEAU, M. and PINARD, A.', *The Development of the Concept of Space in the Child*. New York: International Universities Press.

PIAGET, J. and INHELDER, B. (1948) *The Child's Conception of Space*. London: Routledge and Kegan Paul. (English translation published 1956.)

PIAGET, J. and INHELDER, B. (1969) *The Psychology of the Child*. London: Routledge and Kegan Paul.

ROTMAN, B. (1978) *Jean Piaget: Psychologist of the Real*. Hassocks, Sussex: Harvester Press.

2

A discussion of some issues raised by Piaget's concept of childhood egocentrism

GEORGE BUTTERWORTH

'Intellectual egocentrism has so often been given a meaning quite different from the one we attribute to this word (an ill chosen one no doubt ...)' PIAGET (1959, p. xxiii)

Introduction

More than 50 years have passed since Piaget (1926) first proposed 'egocentrism' to be the defining characteristic of language and thought in the child, yet the meaning and utility of the concept are still being questioned. The purpose of this discussion is both to provide a general background for other chapters in the book and to re-examine the concept in the light of recent experimental evidence, especially as it relates to the origins of egocentrism in infancy.

The chapter begins by closely examining Piaget's definitions. He does not use the term to refer to a personality trait, nor is it an unchanging attribute of childish thought. Egocentrism is defined by undifferentiation between aspects of self and aspects of the physical or social environment and this 'adualism' takes different forms as development proceeds. Having established how the concept is defined and applied, the discussion moves on to consider two topics that have been the occasion for major disagreements over the significance of egocentrism. These are the controversies between Piaget and Vygotsky over 'egocentric speech' and between Piaget and Wallon over 'imitation'. The topics were selected because they serve both to illustrate the subtlety of Piaget's thinking and to pinpoint the weakest part of his theory, namely the relationship between perception and egocentrism. The last part of the chapter examines Piaget's assumption that egocentrism has its roots in a state of total undifferentiation between the human infant and the environment. There is evidence that the infant perceives self motion and appreciates differences between points of view, both supposedly non-egocentric abilities. In each case, the infant perceives a distinction between self and the environment, even though the baby is not self-consciously aware of the distinction. The chapter ends by considering the implications of these findings for theories of egocentrism. Perception is necessarily 'egocentric', in the sense that it originates at a particular viewpoint. However, this need not preclude some kind of awareness of the objective properties of physical and social reality from the earliest stage in development.

By proceeding in this step-wise fashion, I hope to illustrate the concept and points of disagreement, so that what is valuable in the notion, viz. that objective knowledge of self and knowledge of the physical and social environment are correlative, may be retained, without subscribing to the whole of Piaget's theory.

Defining childhood egocentrism

Perhaps the easiest way to grasp the essentials of Piaget's definition is to consider the following quotation:

> Egocentrism denotes a cognitive state in which the cognizer sees the world from a single point of view only, his own but without knowledge of the existence of viewpoints or perspectives and *a fortiori*, without awareness that hc is a prisoner of his own (viewpoint) ... the egocentric subject is a kind of solipsist aware neither of self nor solipsism (Flavell, 1963, p. 60 condensed from Piaget, 1954).

It is clear that in its most fundamental sense, egocentrism has a spatial component based on unwittingly taking the self as the origin of all spatial coordinates and a pre-social component characterized by lack of awareness of the experience or knowledge of others, with a reciprocal lack of self knowledge. Further characteristics of egocentrism can be gleaned from a Piagetian dictionary of quotations (Battro, 1973, pp. 51–54) of which the following are a selection:

(i) It is somehow the totality of precritical and preobjective attitudes of knowledge.
(ii) It is opposed to objectivity as far as objectivity means relativity on the physical plane and reciprocity on the social plane.
(iii) Undifferentiation between the other and the self.
(iv) It consists only in taking as sole reality the one which appears to perception.

These further definitions suggest that Piaget's use of the term is intended to convey *lack of differentiation* between the self and the physical or social environment. Lack of differentiation has its roots in lack of *objective knowledge*, with consequent reliance on the fallible and self-centred impressions of immediate experience. Finally it may be appropriate to include a quotation from Piaget that makes it clear what the term 'egocentrism' *is not* intended to convey.

> I have used the term to designate the initial inability to decenter, to shift the given cognitive perspective. It might have been better to say simply 'Centrism' but since the initial centering of perspective is always relative to one's own

position and action, I said 'egocentrism' and pointed out that the unconscious egocentrism stems from a lack of differentiation between one's own point of view and other possible ones and not at all from an individualism that precedes relations with others (Piaget, 1962, p. 4).

Thus Piaget makes it clear that intellectual egocentrism stands midway between individualized and socialized thought. It is not to be equated with 'selfishness' or a monopolar theoretical orientation focused solely on individual or social aspects of cognitive processes. Given these criteria it should now be clear why Piaget maintains that it is impossible at any level to separate completely the knowing subject from the object that is known: 'These relationships may be more or less centred (on the subject) or decentred and it is this inversion of direction which makes up the transition from subjectivity to objectivity' (Battro, 1973).

At each stage of development, the defining criteria of egocentrism remain constant, although it is manifest in different ways. This repetitive aspect of egocentrism is essential, since cognitive development is thought to proceed by the reacquisition at progressively more abstract levels, of mental operations first acquired at the level of overt activity during infancy. The theory will not be presented in detail here as several alternative sources are readily available (notably Flavell, 1963, Phillips, 1975, and an appendix to Donaldson, 1978). Instead, a brief account will be presented that concentrates on the characteristics of egocentrism at each developmental stage. Specific criticisms of Piaget's theory will be left for later sections of the chapter.

Piaget's theory

The sensorimotor period, ontological egocentrism (0 to 18 months)

Piaget's theory rests on a number of assumptions about the starting point for intellectual development. He ascribes a state of 'radical egocentrism' to the neonate, defined by complete adualism or lack of differentiation between self and world. Although various automatic processes ensure conservation of the biological integrity of the infant, e.g. cell renewal, excretion, etc., at the psychological level there is no conservation of experience. According to Piaget, the only form of predictable continuity is that imposed on reality by inbuilt, reflex actions. Hence the world appears to the infant as a series of 'perceptual tableaux', lacking in permanence, substantiality, constancy of shape or size or spatio-temporal identity. These 'tableaux' appear and reapppear and to the infant seem to be engendered by his own activity. Sensorimotor development lies in the coordination of patterns of action into more and more complex motor programmes that progressively take into account the objective properties of reality. In this theory the infant gradually comes to separate events that are contingent on his own actions from events and objects whose existence is independent of action.

Thus, egocentrism in the sensorimotor period is defined by a 'magical' understanding of causality, in which events appear to the infant to centre on his own activity. Perhaps the most striking example is the stage IV error (Bremner, Chapter 3) (see note at the end of this chapter): Having retrieved a hidden object from its initial location, the infant of eight to 12 months searches again at that location, despite having just seen the same object being hidden at a new place. The object has no identity of its own, no identity independent of the action which was successful in restoring it to immediate experience. Only with the acquisition of the 'concept of the permanent object' at about 18 months does the infant comprehend the spatio-temporal identity of objects and reciprocally becomes aware of himself as just one object among many. The object concept is the first form of conservation in thought and its acquisition completely reverses the infant's initial egocentric perspective on the causal properties of his own activity. The infant now *perceives* his own activities as inserted into an external reality, rather than as engendering that reality.

To summarize, Piaget makes two major assumptions that define the radical egocentrism of infancy and which consequently influence the whole of the rest of his theory. First, the infant is assumed incapable of *directly perceiving* the objective properties of reality. Perception only acquires objectivity when it is mediated by knowledge and knowledge cannot be gained directly through perception. Second, all knowledge, be it of the animate or of the inanimate, is ultimately rooted in individual sensorimotor action patterns. The social world has an *objective existence* (as opposed to being subjectively experienced) only in so far as it is assimilable to individual cognitive processes. For all these reasons, Piaget's formulation can be considered a 'radical egocentrism', rather than simple naïveté, since actions and independent events are not distinguished. The path of development is *necessarily* from the individual to the social because all knowledge is ultimately mediated by the actions of the individual in *constructing* a physical and social reality. (For a full account of Piaget's theory of sensorimotor development there is no better source than the original (1951, 1953, 1954) although Wolff (1960) and DéCarie (1965) offer good short syntheses and Butterworth (1978) offers a detailed critique).

The preoperational period or period of egocentric thought (18 months to eight years)

With the acquisition of the object concept or 'first invariant' of thought, the period of 'ontological egocentricity' (Piaget, 1937) gives way to a new stage. In the pre-operational period mental actions take place on a representation of reality, in lieu of the overt activity of infancy. Even though the child now comes into possession of a language, itself a creation of the social world, this does not ensure objectivity in thinking. Although there is continuity between sensorimotor actions and pre-operational thought because the latter is derived from the former, there is also a discontinuity. Egocentrism, previously overcome at the level of action, now characterizes language and thought. Thus, the preoperational period can be defined as a stage of logical and social egocentricity in which immediate experience dominates rational deduction.

One example of this recapitulation (vertical *décalage*) is the child's inability to appreciate any perspective save his own in spatial reasoning tasks (see Cox, Chapter 4). Although by 12 months the baby *perceives* constancy of shape and size of an object under its own manual transformations, the child of four or five years is unable to *conceive* of such invariant properties. For example, Piaget's children, on a walk around a mountain, seem convinced that changes in apparent size or shape of the mountain seen from different perspectives are quite real. The child is said to be dominated by immediate experience: 'Objects are assimilated to the ego on the model of its own activity' (Piaget, 1937).

Hence, preoperational thought is 'anthropometric' or 'animistic' because events are understood only in relation to the child's limited comprehension of self. The conceptual world is centred on the child's own ego and, as such, thought leads to 'satisfaction rather than objectivity' (Piaget, 1954, p. 362). A similar animistic quality is observed in the child's play where thoughts may remain 'strictly individual and incommunicable' (1954, p. 362). With respect to the child's speech, Piaget (1926) goes so far as to derive a coefficient of egocentrism. Of 1500 remarks made by a six-year-old child and recorded over a period of one month, almost half is described as 'egocentric speech'. Egocentric speech is defined as monologue (where the child speaks without apparently addressing anyone), collective monologue (talking aloud to the self but in front of others) and repetition (playing with words – see Robinson and Robinson, Chapter 6). Piaget concludes:

It would seem that up to a certain age, we may safely admit that children think and act more egocentrically than adults, that they share each other's intellectual life less than we do. True, when they are together they seem to talk to each other a great deal more than we do about what they are doing but for the most part, they are only talking to themselves. We on the contrary keep silent for longer about our action, but our talk is almost always socialized (1926, reprinted in Dennis, 1972).

The period of concrete operations or rational thought (eight to 12 years)

According to Piaget, the emergence of rational thought depends both on the coordination of perspectives by the individual and on the coordination of the individual's own perspective with those of others. Thus, *social coordination is* a necessary condition for logical thinking: 'The essence of rational coordination is to be sought in the fundamental group of operations which ensure the reciprocity of individual perspectives and the relativity of the facts of experience' (Piaget, 1937, p. 45).

For example, in the child's developing conception of space, left and right are initially treated as absolutes. However, the child eventually understands that his own left corresponds to the right of an individual opposite him, a relative and reciprocal spatial relationship. Essentially, this cognitive advance comes about because the child coordinates individual perspectives into a unitary concept of space. The child's conceptual knowledge becomes superimposed on his previous level of understanding, which was merely 'practical', i.e. defined by transformations occurring under his own activity. Similar principles underlie the acquisition of concepts such as conservation of volume or weight and class inclusion. The individual, perceptible, properties of objects, e.g. the height and width of the liquid in a conservation task, are coordinated into a systematic, reversible system defined by the invariant properties of the substance undergoing transformation. 'In any field, the faculty of knowing is a process of coordination in which the ego is subordinated to some objective system of reference and the logic of relationships is nothing but a tool and the result of this coordination' (1937, p. 48).

In summary, the child's 'escape from egocentricism' lies firstly in the coordination of actions in infancy, hence to impose an invariant structure on the world. This is followed by a period of egocentric thought in which the coordinations established at the level of action must be reestablished conceptually. Coordinated internalized actions (known as operations) mark the onset of the concrete operational period and a logic defined by reciprocal and reversible relationships. Hence the child's actions are at one and the same time the *source* of egocentricity and the means by which it becomes transcended. Socialization also depends on cooperation and reciprocity in personal relationships. In infancy, reciprocity will be established at the level of action, while the conflicting ideas to which the child is exposed in social interaction during the preoperational period will lead to awareness of what is individual to the child's own thinking, by contrast with ideas that are social or agreed.

Formal operations and egocentrism (12 years onwards)

Although with the acquisition of concrete operational thought the naïve egocentrism of childhood is overcome, egocentric thinking can nevertheless be observed throughout life. Formal operations are second-order reasoning processes that permit the individual to 'think about thinking', a transition from the intrapropositional logic of concrete operations to an interpropositional logic. This marks yet another reversal of perspective since now the child *first* considers abstract possibilities and tests them against concrete reality, rather than *deriving* abstract invariants from concrete reality as in the preceding stage.

Elkind (1978) has catalogued some egocentric errors that occur through failure to differentiate what is objective and what is subjective at the level of abstract thought. For example, the self-consciousness of the adolescent is attributed to failure to recognize that real or imagined 'flaws' in appearance are not necessarily of any great consequence to others. Another example is given of failure to distinguish experiences that are universal from experiences that are unique, as in the case of the infatuated young woman who tells her mother: 'You don't know how it feels to be in love'. Piaget (1962, p. 5) also gives an example (which may be apocryphal): A young university teacher delivers his first lecture only to discover that no one understands what he is talking about. This is an example of 'egocentric speech', since the teacher fails to take into account the lesser knowledge of the students and consequently speaks 'over their heads'.

In summary, egocentrism is defined as a state of undifferentiation between self and environment, manifest in different ways at various stages of development. In its earliest form, the infant fails to differentiate between the effects of his own actions and independent events, consequently acquiring a false perspective on self and the relationship between action and objects. With the development of memory and the capacity to represent reality during the preoperational period, there is a reversal of this initial perspective and the young child now understands perceived reality to be independent of action and the self to be one object among many. However, thought remains tied to the child's own perspective and he fails to differentiate between the variant and the invariant properties of substance under transformation. With the acquisition of concrete operations, thought takes on the property of reversibility, the child is no longer dominated by the appearance of things and the reciprocity of different points of view is understood, so long as thinking occurs with respect to concrete problems. The child can reason objectively about physical and social events and hence self and others are further differentiated within the limits of concrete thought. The acquisition of formal operations, the ability to 'think about thinking' marks yet another reversal in the child's perspective on reality; abstract deductions can now be tested against concrete evidence. Nevertheless, even the adult sometimes fails to differentiate what is public from what is private knowledge and to the extent that this occurs, egocentrism can be observed throughout life.

It is difficult to deny that the general concept of 'egocentrism', as a characteristic of thought lacking in objectivity, captures familiar qualities of childhood intellectual processes. However, it is not with its descriptive usefulness but with its explanatory status that major disagreements have arisen. In the next section, we will examine some objections to the concept and Piaget's replies to his critics.

Controversies over the significance of childhood egocentrism

It should be clear by now that egocentrism is defined by lack of differentiation, whether between action and object, the individual and the social, the private and the public or the subjective and the objective. This is assumed to have its roots in the radical adualism of early infancy, an assumption that has rarely been questioned.

Instead, controversies rage around the direction of developmental change, whether development proceeds from the individual to the social or from the social to the individual. In this section it will become apparent that such controversies often boil down to arguments about the relative merits of alternative sides of the same coin, although to be sure, different emphases focus attention on different aspects of the developmental process.

Piaget and Vygotsky on egocentric speech

Perhaps the best known controversy and the one that sets the issues in the clearest light, is the debate between Piaget and Vygotsky over the role of egocentric speech in the development of thinking. (It is a little inaccurate to call it a debate because there was a gap of 28 years between the first publication in 1934 of Vygotsky's (1962) criticisms and Piaget's (1962) reply and the whole exchange took place after Vygotsky's death.)

To understand this debate, it is necessary to state the ways in which Piaget's structuralist theory and Vygotsky's approach based on Soviet materialist dialectics are similar (see Wozniak, 1975). Both theories are interactionist, in that reality modifies structures inherent in a developing organism, both emphasize subject–object relations, both emphasize the actions of the subject in the construction of knowledge, and, in both theories, knowledge of reality becomes more adequate with development. Where the theories differ is in the aspect of the interaction which is regarded as primary for purposes of theory building. Piaget accords primacy to the subject because he is interested in continuities between biological and psychological adaptation and, in particular, in deriving the structures of scientific thought from their origins in individual actions. In the Soviet theory, on the other hand, primacy is accorded to the material and social environment. Language is considered a particularly important feature of the human social environment both as a cultural mediator of reality and as an essential instrument for self-regulation of behaviour.

The different predispositions of the authors lead to different foci in their respective theories. Piaget traces the development of cognitive structures (strictly speaking he is interested in the epistemic subject, a fictional average) and consequently he focuses on the constructive role of the subject in intellectual development, language acquisition, socialization and the whole process of learning. Vygotsky on the other hand focuses on the relation of the social to the individual, with consequently greater emphasis on the cultural transmission of knowledge, teaching and the role of language in thinking.

The debate between Piaget and Vygotsky followed Vygotsky's criticisms of Piaget's theory of egocentric speech. To recapitulate, Piaget found that roughly 50% of the speech of preschool children (always bearing in mind the particular situation) does not result in any *effective communication* with others. As Piaget

(1962) points out, it is not that the speech was not *meant for* others but that the child talks *for himself*, in the sense that the university lecturer of our previous example also failed to communicate. Piaget believes that the decline in egocentric speech during the concrete operational period occurs because the child acquires the intellectual operations of reciprocity necessary for effective communication. He did not accord egocentric speech any further importance in his theory.

Vygotsky, proceeding from the social plane to the individual, saw egocentric speech as a transitional stage between a global communication function that is necessarily at first shared (since language can only be acquired in a social context) and verbal thought or inner speech. By starting from a social perspective on individual cognitive processes Vygotsky drew attention to an important developmental continuity between overt speech and verbal thought in planning and regulating action. Piaget (1962) gives him credit for this discovery but this does not alter his opinion that failure to differentiate what is social from what is individual is the main obstacle to rational coordination of viewpoints and effective communication.

In the light of Piaget's (1962) detailed discussion of Vygotsky's criticisms it is difficult to continue to place the two approaches completely in opposition. Nevertheless, there are aspects of the debate that deserve further consideration. One issue is highlighted by Vygotsky's insistence on the role of language in cognition. Piaget's emphasis has always been to make language secondary to intellectual operations in the development of thinking, whereas language might be considered an aspect of the cognitive system, in its own right. Karmilloff-Smith (1979) has suggested that from its inception, language may serve not only as a tool for representing something already known but also it becomes part of the 'cognitive economy', something the child not only thinks about but also thinks with. One reason for re-emphasizing the role of language in the preoperational period is that it may be a more parsimonious way of representing reality than is afforded by visual imagery. Another reason is that it would be strange from an evolutionary point of view, if the capacity for language merely duplicates mechanisms for acquiring knowledge in other ways. To be sure, there must be continuity between prelinguistic and linguistic structures, but the structural approach may underestimate the functional utility of a specifically human way of knowing. It remains to be seen whether the capacity for language is rooted in sensorimotor action schemes, in social interaction, in both or in some other shared property of human cognition (see Bruner and Garton, 1978).

A second aspect of the debate that deserves further consideration, concerns the role of instruction, or cultural transmission of knowledge. Vygotsky (1962, p. 116) took Piaget to task for underestimating the importance of teaching in cognitive development, particularly with respect to the acquisition of scientific concepts. Piaget's analysis is said also to underestimate the intellectual capacities of the preschool child (probably because his stress on egocentrism inevitably tends to emphasize intellectual limitations). Vygotsky argues that the preschool child's thought is much more rational in the 'spontaneous concepts' acquired in everyday life, than in 'abstract concepts' related to scientific knowledge. For example, a child's concept of his 'brother' is rich, vital, multi-faceted and defined by the intersection of a variety of experiences, even though the child may lack a precise ability to define the concept in words. Hence, when Piaget questions the child about his 'brother's brother' he obtains answers that suggest a lack of reciprocity. The child fails to understand himself to be his brother's brother. Nevertheless, in some sense he has the concept, although he cannot at will define it or manipulate it intellectually.

Vygotsky likens the acquisition of *abstract scientific concepts* to the learning of a foreign language. This requires deliberate, conscious activity, since such concepts initially lack content and are 'filled in' through schooling, reading and deliberate instruction. However, the acquisition of *scientific knowledge* is Piaget's major preoccupation, so the important question in evaluating Vygotsky's criticism is the relationship in development between the preschool child's spontaneous concepts and the abstract, scientific concepts that will be taught in school. Vygotsky expresses himself simply; spontaneous concepts create a developmental pathway for the acquisition of scientific concepts. The content-filled, 'spontaneous' concept gradually becomes more abstract, until eventually it provides an anchoring point for the acquisition of abstract, culturally transmitted concepts.

As Piaget (1962) makes clear, there is no fundamental incompatibility between these views and his own. With respect to teaching and learning, Piaget points out that his major concern is that information transmitted to the child should be tailored to the child's stage of intellectual development, if the child is to benefit. With respect to the distinction between 'spontaneous' and 'scientific' concepts, Piaget agrees that there must be a point where the intellectual development of the individual has proceeded sufficiently to absorb culturally transmitted knowledge. He argues that the critical question is how the child becomes *aware* of the abstract relations implicit in the spontaneous concepts which form the basis of scientific thought. The egocentric, preschool child is aware of the *results* of an action or of the content of a concept but has no awareness of the *operations* governing an action or of the *relations* implicit in the concept. Decentering, or the shift from an egocentric perspective, leads to an awareness of the operations themselves and a consequent abstraction of their essential properties.

These issues have been discussed in some detail because it may be the case that the debate between Piaget and Vygotsky is at present being recapitulated. Donaldson (1978) levels exactly the same criticisms at Piaget as Vygotsky did 40 years previously. She argues that Piaget's abstract tasks do not make 'human sense' to the preschool child, they are not encompassed by everyday experience and hence sadly overestimate the young child's egocentrism. When tasks are presented in such a way that motives and intentions are comprehensible, so that the child can act in a way compatible with familiar social experiences then there is exhibited competence in perspective-taking, class-inclusion, conservation and other forms of logical reasoning, not usually found before the period of concrete operations. The experiments Donaldson cites are ingenious and they do indeed add a new dimension to the traditional Piagetian analysis of reasoning tasks. However, whether they demonstrate that the preschool child is capable of concrete operational reasoning, as Donaldson seems to claim, or simply a continuity between preoperational *judgements* and *concrete operational thought* is a matter for dispute.

The first example is an ingenious investigation of number conservation (McGarrigle and Donaldson, 1974/5). Part of the procedure followed the standard Piagetian method. Two rows of four counters were placed in one to one correspondence so that the rows were of equal length and each counter was opposite another. (A task with unequal numbers of elements was also used but the 'equality' task will be taken as our example.) The preschool child is asked whether there are the same number of counters in each row, and will readily assent that there are. Then the adult lengthens one of the rows by redistributing the counters and the child is again asked whether there are the same number of counters in each row. Typically, the child changes his judgement and says there are more in the longer row (only 15/80 children aged four to six years were correct).

McGarrigle and Donaldson compared performance on the standard task with a condition in which a 'naughty teddy' 'accidentally' transformed the array so that its final appearance was exactly as in the standard conservation task. When asked if the numbers of elements were the same or different, 50/80 children were now correct. The authors suggest that in the standard task the adult's intentional activity draws the child's attention to the irrelevant attribute (length), by which the child interprets the adult's questions about number. In the accidental situation, the child is not distracted by the irrelevant attribute and goes on to give the correct answer, demonstrating 'conservation'. The authors argue that 'inability to decentre' (i.e. egocentrism) cannot explain these results, since the perceptual properties of the array are identical in both cases. It is only when the equality question occurs in conjunction with the adult's intentional action that children fail to conserve. McGarrigle and Donaldson argue that the adult's intentional activity provides a context or setting, by which the child interprets the adult's question. If the experimenter's behaviour indicates that length *is* a relevant attribute, then the child interprets the questions accordingly. The child needs a 'dictionary', something outside the language itself, to be able to grasp the meaning of the utterance.

There is every reason to suppose this aspect of the argument to be true but it surely follows that if the extra-linguistic context is the means by which the child interprets adults' questions about the perceptual transformation, this must apply *equally* to the intentional *and* the accidental transformation. It cannot be argued that the intentional nature of the adult's activity 'is at variance with the meaning of the utterance', (1974/5, p. 347) if the extra-linguistic context is *precisely* what gives meaning to the utterance. Rather than argue that the child is in possession of the concept at a linguistic level in one context but not in the other (and it is surely at the linguistic level that the concept becomes 'scientific' rather than 'spontaneous' in Vygotsky's terms) it would be more parsimonious to argue that neither correct nor incorrect performance are indicative of concrete operational reasoning. Instead, one might wish to turn attention to the possibility that there exists a form of conservation at the *perceptual level*, i.e. the child may be able to perceive directly the invariance of number, just as 18-month-old infants seem able to perceive the invariance of weight under a transformation (Mounoud and Bower, 1974). The problem for the child is to *perceive* from the experimenter's actions whether the adult's language refers to the variant attributes of the display (in this case length) or the invariant attributes of the display. The *intentional act* is the child's only clue to the referent of the utterance and this picks out length as the criterial attribute of number. In the 'accidental' condition, where there is no direct reference to the variant or the invariant properties of the display in the experimenter's non-verbal behaviour, the meaning of his question might be translated in terms of the perceived invariant properties of the display. It is not unreasonable to stress the *perceptual* competence of preschool children in a variety of logical reasoning tasks (Bryant, 1974), so this could explain McGarrigle and Donaldson's results.

The second example concerns the ability of preschool children to take the perspective of another. Donaldson (1978) quotes a study by Hughes that suggests children as young as three years may be able to work out what somebody else can see from a position different from their own. The child's task was to place a boy doll at one of four positions formed by the intersection of two screens, so that two 'policemen' dolls could not see the boy doll. In other words, the doll had to be placed in such a position that the screens formed a barrier to the perception of the doll by the 'policemen' (the task is fully described in Cox, Chapter 4). Donaldson argues that children found this task easy because it made 'human sense', the action of hiding is easy for the child to understand in simple human terms. As Cox makes clear in her chapter, however, getting this task right does not necessarily require the complex operational abilities involved in describing a scene from the perspective of another observer. There are a whole set of qualitative changes in development between the elementary ability to make use of another person's line of regard and the complex ability of constructing a visual image of a scene from another perspective. The important question, in terms of evaluating Piaget's theory of childhood egocentrism, is whether the ability to hide an object from another person is an extension of the ability already acquired in infancy to find a hidden object. If merely an elementary level of representation is required, then Hughes' findings are not necessarily incompatible with Piaget's theory. The general question of how young children are able to follow another person's line of regard will be taken up again towards the end of this chapter.

What have these examples to offer on the wider issue of childhood egocentrism? If, as Donaldson argues, the meaning of an utterance is not differentiated from its context, this would appear to meet one of the criterial attributes of egocentrism. Similarly, if the child can *perceive* invariance of number (even though he cannot conceive of it), the world is what it appears to the child's perception and even a successful solution might be described as 'egocentric'. However, the latter statement begins to depart from Piaget's definition because now an *objective* property of reality is known through perception, as opposed to Piaget's assumption that perception is necessarily distorting. Thus, it may be fruitful to examine the role of *perception* in cognitive development, if the concept of egocentrism is to be reformulated. The following discussion may lead us further in this direction.

Piaget and Wallon on imitation

Henri Wallon (1879–1962) is not widely known in the English-speaking world, although he has had a great influence on French and European psychology. He trained as a physician and paediatrician and was concerned with both normal and abnormal development. Like Vygotsky, he approached cognitive development from a social perspective and there are many points of agreement between his and Piaget's theories (Birns, 1973; Voyat, 1973) as well as some points of disagreement. Disagreements arose over the roles of language, emotion and imitation in cognitive development (Wallon, 1973a, b and c). It is on imitation that we will focus here because it offers further insights into the nature of egocentrism.

Social imitation may be defined as putting one's own actions into correspondence with those of another person. Facial imitation has been taken as a particularly important landmark in cognitive development, because it involves using a part of the body one cannot see and hence Piaget (1951) considered it not to be an aspect of immediate perception. Simply stated, imitation proceeds from imitation of self to imitation of others. The infant begins to imitate by repeating actions involving parts of the body that are visible (primary and secondary circular reactions) without awareness that the stimulus giving rise to his activity is external to the action. Facial imitation begins at around 12 months and develops with the capacity to represent (i.e. hold in mind) events which take place out of sight.

In Wallon's account, imitation is social from the outset, i.e. it is imitation of another. Initially, imitation occurs without the infant being aware that he is imitating. This phenomenon Wallon calls 'participation' or 'pseudo-imitation' and it is said to occur in an early 'symbiotic' stage of infancy. Later, from about 12 months onwards, 'real (deliberate or intentional) imitation' begins.

The critical test between these theories lies in the genesis of facial imitation. For

Wallon there is no reason why it should not occur early in life, whereas for Piaget it is excluded since the *perception* of facial correspondence requires the infant first to *construct* the correspondence through actions. (Specifically, Piaget argues that the infant discovers the correspondence by touching an adult's face, then his own and inferring perceptual similarity from the tactual similarity.)

Although there have been previous reports that infants can imitate specific facial acts, such as tongue protrusion in the first three months (McDougall, 1928; Guillaume, 1971) it is only recently that precise experiments have been carried out. Maratos (1974) found that infants can imitate tongue protrusion between two and six weeks of age. This research has been replicated by Meltzoff and Moore (1977) who found that imitation of tongue protrusion can occur in the first day of life. These results suggest that there exist mechanisms of cross modal correspondence that are available to the infant from the outset, and this has important consequences for Piaget's theory (see Butterworth 1980). From the point of view of the origins of egocentrism, they may suggest a different hypothesis to the 'radical adualism' proposed by Piaget.

Both Piaget and Wallon emphasize differentiation as a mechanism of cognitive development. For Piaget, however, development starts with a complete lack of differentiation in which the infant experiences the world as an extension of action. Wallon's 'symbiotic stage' of early infancy implies a *preestablished harmony* between infant and environment, rather than an adualistic confusion. Perhaps a concrete example may make the distinction clearer. Consider the symbiotic relation between the cleaner fish and the shark. It is not the case that fish and shark are undifferentiated in each other's perception, since the whole delicate relationship depends on precise discriminations, signals, etc. What defines symbiosis is the mutual dependence of the parties; their separate behaviours are best understood as complementary aspects of a total system.

By the same token, the relations into which a neonate enters with both its physical and social environment must be the point from which all development will proceed but these relationships need not be characterized by a *total* lack of differentiation. It is quite possible that there may exist a prereflective level of awareness, where perception is differentiated into a subject–object pole, even though the infant is not aware of self as subject (Bolton, 1978). If egocentrism consists in 'taking as sole reality the one which appears to perception' (Piaget, in Battro, 1973) it becomes important to establish whether infant perception is characterized by lack of differentiation, or whether subject–object distinctions are present albeit at an elementary level.

Perception in infancy and the definition of egocentrism

Piaget makes perception subordinate to action in his theory of sensorimotor development. Knowledge is obtained through action and this gives structure to perception. A great deal of evidence has now accumulated against Piaget's theory of infant perception (see Butterworth, 1978, 1980), so this section will be limited to brief discussions of the infant's perception of self and the infant's perception of another's line of regard. Both of these topics are directly related to the question of egocentrism and its origins.

The infant's perception of self motion

Piaget's theory of infant visual perception retains the empiricist assumption that visual stimulation at the two-dimensional surface of the retina is insufficient to specify directly a three-dimensional extended space. It is not until the infant acquires the 'object concept' at about 18 months that sensory stimulation is interpreted according to its objective properties. The object concept mediates the child's perception and allows him to differentiate events that are contingent on action from events that are independent of action. It also implies knowledge of self, said to be required to overcome the adualism of the sensorimotor period. In summary, Piaget proposes a *mediated* theory of perception: sensory input only acquires meaningful structure in relation to the infant's capacity to act instrumentally and impose spatial and temporal order on experience.

J. J. Gibson (1966) has long opposed such theories of perception. He argues that the retinal image should not be considered a 'picture' of reality requiring interpretation but as a surface containing information that directly specifies the objective properties of reality. He argues that the *world* is structured by objects set on textured surfaces and that reflected light preserves environmentally invariant information at the retina, sufficient both to specify directly the objective properties of the environment *and* properties of the perceiving organism. The particular example which concerns us here is the perception of self motion. According to Gibson, perspectival transformations of the two-dimensional retinal array are sufficient to specify movement of an observer through a three-dimensional space. Under ecologically valid conditions, an expanding flow pattern of the whole textured retinal image can only occur when the observer is moving forward, relative to a stable external space. Since this is an invariant relation, the observer can directly perceive that he is in motion toward the stationary central point at the focus of optical expansion. The information at the retina has an objective and a subjective pole built in, sufficient to distinguish motion of self from motion of the environment.

Lee and Aronson (1974) showed that infants use visual information to monitor their posture when they first stand unsupported. This was demonstrated by standing the infants on a stable floor inside a 'moveable room' comprising three walls and a ceiling. The infants face the interior end wall of the room and the whole structure, except the stable floor, was moved so that the end wall approached or receded. Babies compensated for a non-existent loss of balance and they consequently swayed, staggered or fell in a direction appropriate to the misleading visual feedback. For example, if the end wall moved away from the infant, thus providing information consistent with backward loss of stability, the babies compensated and fell forward. Infants perceived the visual information to specify self motion, exactly as Gibson would expect.

This effect of discrepant visual feedback does not arise through acquisition of the upright stance. Butterworth and Hicks (1977) compared the stability of the seated posture in infants who could *sit unsupported but not stand* with infants who could *sit or stand* unsupported. The younger infants, who had not yet learned to stand, compensated at least as intensely for a visually specified loss of stability as the older group who could stand. Therefore the infant's response to the visual information was not learned through the motor activity of learning to stand. In a subsequent experiment (Butterworth and Cicchetti, 1978), the role of motor experience in establishing control over posture was examined. Sitting and standing under conditions of discrepant visual feedback were compared in normal infants and motor-retarded Down's syndrome babies. A consistent *decline* in the intensity of response to movement of the surround was correlated with increasing experience of the respective postures. Far from motor activity slowly giving structure to the visual flow pattern, all the evidence suggested that infants actually make use of the invariant properties of the visual flow pattern to gain control over posture. (See also Butterworth, 1980). Even the motor-retarded Down's syndrome infants responded to discrepant visual feedback in the same way as normals when learning to stand.

We can be sure that these effects of misleading visual feedback on posture are not learned through locomotor activities, since the youngest sitting infants were not able to crawl, yet they showed strong responses to the movement of the whole surround. If such postural compensations to visually specified instability prove to be innate, it would imply that the perceptual system has, over evolutionary time, come to anticipate the pattern of optic flow that is contingent on self movement. The relationship between organism and environment can be considered a feedback control loop in which self motion is specified in the optic flow pattern, so that even under conditions of passive movement, the distinction between observer and environment would be imposed on the infant by the natural ecology.

The experiments made it clear, however, that even though the visual information may *specify* self movement (i.e. provide objective information for stability/instability), the infant who has just learned to sit or stand has no *objective knowledge* of self. Under the *ecologically invalid* conditions of the moving room, the infant compensates for a *non-existent* loss of balance, thus betraying lack of self-knowledge. Only after prolonged experience of the standing posture (about 12 months after first standing unsupported) did the babies become sufficiently independent of the visual surround so that they could maintain a stable posture despite movement of the room. At about the same time, they would often laugh and turn behind them to see 'who was making the room move'.

Thus, Gibson may be correct to argue that stimulus information contains invariants that can be apprehended at the level of perception, and that these invariants have a subject and object pole built in. On the other hand, Piaget is also correct to argue that *objective* knowledge of self has a qualitatively different status in development, one that allows the infant to transcend on earlier mode of functioning. The intriguing possibility is that *objective knowledge* of postural stability (a criterion of non-egocentricity since it is an aspect of self-knowledge) may have its origins in prestructured visual feedback which *imposes* a distinction in perception between motion of the infant and motion of the environment. Although the infant's postural compensations in the 'moving room' situation certainly demonstrate lack of differentiation from the surround, this is only because the stability of the infant and the stability of the environment under *ecologically valid* conditions, are complementary aspects of a total system, with an *implicit* subject–object distinction. The problem in development is to make the implicit distinction explicit not to *give rise* to the distinction *de novo*.

The infant's perception of another's point of view

We can now extend this line of argument into the social realm. A phenomenon that bears directly on Piaget's theory of infant egocentrism is the capacity of even very young infants to attend jointly to the environment with an adult. Scaife and Bruner (1975) showed that infants from two months of age will adjust their line of gaze in response to a change in the focus of attention of an adult. These results suggest that babies must be less than totally egocentric since they seem to take into account the point of view of *another* person in order to reorient their own visual attention.

Butterworth and Cochran (1979) carried out a series of experiments in order to try to establish the mechanism underlying the capacity for joint visual attention in infancy. Subjects were babies aged between six and 18 months and their mothers. The experiments took place in a small room, with mother and baby seated opposite each other in the centre of the laboratory. Pairs of targets were presented at various positions arranged to their left and right. This is schematized in Figure 1.

The mother was instructed to interact naturally with her baby and when she felt sure the infant's attention was on her, to turn and inspect one of the targets in the room. Targets were usually presented in pairs (1 and 2, 5 and 6, etc.) and the procedure was repeated until the mother had looked at all the locations. The most striking result was that between six and 18 months infants *hardly ever* succeeded in locating a target behind them (locations 1, 2, 3, 4 in Figure 1). When the mother fixated a target in that region of space, infants would turn in the appropriate direction but they would scan the space in *front of them* up to a visual angle of about

33

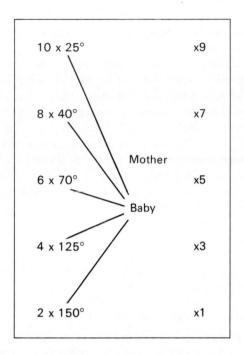

Fig. 1: Target locations and laboratory layout (Butterworth and Cochran, 1979)
1 to 10: Target locations (a subset of targets was presented at any one trial)
Approximate visual angles of targets with respect to baby are shown.

40° (where locations 7, 8, 9 and 10 would have been). On the other hand, for targets within the infants' visual field, they were perfectly capable of localizing positions as extreme as 70° (5 and 6). That is, if the nearest target was at 125° from the infant, they would terminate their scan at 40°, even though they were perfectly capable of reorienting their attention to targets displaced up to 70° from the midline.

These results suggested that visual reorientation may occur as a two-step process: first, the infant may turn about 40° from the midline, so that the mother is in the extreme periphery of vision to one side; then, if a target appears in the periphery of vision to the other side, the infant will foveate it. If these conditions are not met by the presence of a target in the periphery, the infant usually terminates the head and eye movement at about 40°, at the point where the mother leaves the visual field. The mother, a possible referent of her action and the infant must be momentarily connected *in the infants own visual space*, before the infant will foveate the peripheral target.

The fact that infants respond at all to the adult's change of gaze might suggest non-egocentrism, on the argument that it is the action of another that leads the baby to respond. On the other hand, since under certain circumstances the infant assimilates the mother's objective line of regard to his own visual field, this might be interpreted as evidence for egocentrism (when mother looks behind baby, the infant terminates visual search at 40° if his visual field is empty or when several targets are presented at once the baby picks out a target in front of him). To resolve this paradox, quite a different explanation is required than Piaget's solipsistic theory of infant perception.

A perceptual process such as that described above can resolve the quandary. Perception *necessarily* involves a point of view but this need not preclude an ability to perceive somebody else's perspective on a space common to several points of view. William James expresses the spirit of this argument well:

> Practically then our minds meet in a world of objects which they share in common ... if my reader will only allow that the same dollar goes into his pocket as came out of mine ... that the same 'now' both ends his past and begins his future ... he will also in consistency have to allow that the same object may conceivably play a part in, as being related to, the rest of any number of otherwise unrelated minds (1947, p. 79, first published in 1912).

On James' account, joint visual attention is made possible by inferential processes based on objects held in common and which *exist within a common space*. To respond to objects located in a space which extends beyond the boundaries of immediate perception, e.g. behind the infant, may indeed require *conceptual* knowledge. But a conceptual space may only extend the boundaries of a space already available to the infant in immediate perception; conceptual knowledge may not be a necessary condition for *perceiving* the viewpoint of another. (Such a perceptual process does not literally require the infant to 'place himself in the other's shoes'. It merely requires perception of the general direction of the adult's gaze into the infant's visual space.)

This argument therefore takes us one step further in unravelling the problem of egocentrism. Perception necessarily involves a point of view, i.e. what is perceived is ultimately referred to the perceiver's own perspective, but this need not preclude a reciprocity in attentional processes from an early age. But what is it that allows such a process to occur at the level of perception? It seems likely that the infant perceives the adult's actions against the background that is *at the same time*, the background accessible to the adult's visual perception. An elementary intersubjective process, such as joint visual attention, is only possible because the perceptual systems of different people function in basically the same way. (In turn, this is only true because we have evolved in relation to the same *objective* reality that gives structure to the perceptual system.) In scanning the infant's visual space, the adult is also scanning her own visual space and *vice versa*.

The essence of this argument is that perceptual processes, rather than Piaget's circular reactions, set the upper and lower limits on reciprocity in early social relations. Piaget is probably incorrect to assume that no form of social reciprocity can exist without objective knowledge of the self or of the other person, but he is probably correct to emphasize the role of objective knowledge in extending the contexts through which communication can take place. For example, for the infant to engage in joint visual attention with respect to a space extending beyond immediate visual perception, it would appear necessary that a representation of space must develop. Piaget would also have a great deal more to say about the qualitative changes that will occur in the development of reciprocity, even if he were to grant the neonativist points made above. Reciprocity at the level of infant perception is anchored at the perceiver's end of the relationship, the infant perceives the other's point of view from his own point of view. The reciprocity of the concrete operational period implies a more complex type of reversible relation, i.e. the child can take the other's point of view from the other's position and hence reflect on his own position *vis-à-vis* the other. (I am indebted to Stephen Huggett for pointing out to me two forms of reversible operation: unidirectional and bidirectional in cognitive development.) Joint visual attention is merely the most elementary of a hierarchy of cognitive processes remaining to be developed.

Perception and egocentrism

These examples of infant perceptual competence finally take us to the crux of the problem of egocentrism, namely the relation between perception and the acquisition of knowledge. Perception of self motion, perception of another's point of view and neonatal facial imitation support Gibson's general proposition that perceptual systems function directly in relation to the physical and social environment, without the necessity for conceptual mediation. At the most elementary level of cognitive functioning, before the baby has objective knowledge or self conscious awareness, the distinction between perceiver and perceived may be implicit in perception.

If this hypothesis is accepted, then it becomes necessary to reformulate what is implied in Piaget's definition of egocentrism as 'taking as the sole reality the one which appears to perception'. Piaget implies that perception is private, subjective and somehow incoherent but if perceptual systems have evolved to pick up invariant information directly, then the objective structure of the perceived physical and social world is an aspect of experience potentially available to all. From the outset, the infant participates in, and is intimately linked to, a world that he holds in common with others. An organism that functions at the perceptual level is *necessarily* egocentric, in the sense that perception involves a point of view; as Hamlyn (1978) says, one cannot perceive *but from* a particular point of view. This is not to say that there is initially a privacy or solipsism of experience. Although the infant or young child may largely comprehend reality through direct perceptual experience, the child's experience is of *public* objects. Far from perception being a barrier to the acquisition of objective knowledge, in Piaget's theory the kind of knowledge that can be formulated in the language of scientific description, it is the *consensibility* of perception that provides the key to intersubjective agreement and scientific understanding.

In summary, in Piaget's theory, the objective properties of the world must be constructed before they can be perceived. When the child falls back on his experience, the world as it appears to him, he is being egocentric because on Piaget's model of perception, that experience must lack objectivity and hence cannot be shared or communicated. If Piaget's model of perception is wrong, however, then to fall back on perception where objective knowledge or a sufficiently developed language is lacking, is to fall back on the objective properties of reality, the bedrock on which intersubjective agreement is based.

Conclusion

This approach to the acquisition of knowledge has certain advantages over Piaget's formulation. For example, it more readily explains why the child should be so dependent on contextual information in acquiring and interpreting language. Perceptual processes provide a dictionary outside the language itself, whereby the child can discover the meaning of an utterance. Similarly, in the development of perspective-taking skills, it should come as no surprise that the child is aware that his own point of view changes from different vantage points before he can describe other peoples' points of view (Cox, Chapter 4). Although Piaget is correct to distinguish the former ability from the latter, it is an error to dismiss it as merely a 'practical' kind of understanding. The child understands his own point of view to change because he can directly perceive that it *does* change. To describe another person's point of view requires a certain effort of the imagination and here Piaget may be correct to argue that the ability does not develop until the child has acquired concrete operational reasoning.

The full implications of such an approach to the development of understanding remain to be worked out. It is clear, however, that 'to perceive' is not synonymous with 'to know'. Objective knowledge of self and world introduces a new level of awareness in the child's experience. Distinctions that may be implicit in perception become explicit, the perceiver becomes capable of self-perception. Thus it would be a mistake to dismiss the concept of egocentrism from the psychological vocabulary. It captures an essential correlation between knower and known, between aspects of self and aspects of the physical and social environment. While retaining this component of the concept of egocentrism, it may be time to move beyond the entrenched positions that development proceeds either from the individual level to the social, or from the social level to the individual. The kind of theory that is required is one in which social and individual aspects of psychological functioning stand in mutual dependence so that perception and thought, thought and language, language and scientific knowledge can be understood as interpenetrating influences in development.

Note

I have not discussed Piaget's stage IV error in relation to infant egocentrism in this chapter because I have done so in detail elsewhere – Butterworth, G. E. (Ed.) (1980) *Infancy and Epistemology*. Hassocks, Sussex: Harvester Press. Bremner adequately reviews the published literature and concludes that the infant may not be completely egocentric since the hidden object is located in relation to a visible landmark, rather than in relation to his previous response. However, even this may be compatible with Piaget's argument that the baby is limited in the ability to identify an object experienced successively by a topological concept of space. In such a spatial reference system, relations of proximity determine object localization and this in turn means that the object is identified as 'identical to itself' only at the initial, distinctive location where it was previously found.

A critical test of this theory would be to establish whether there exist spatial conditions under which the infant can search accurately when the object is hidden at *successive* locations and its path of movement is visible. There is evidence that infants can solve the stage IV problem when the successive locations are distinctively different and placed on a continuous surface (Butterworth, 1980). Thus, the spatial relation between the object and its *background* may be one critical factor influencing the pattern of search. In my own experiments, where the surface is continuous and structured with distinctively different covers, babies search accurately at the old and the new location, even though this requires them to make a new response to a distinctively different cover. In Bremner's studies, the object is hidden in a well sunk into the table surface and infants make perseverative errors to the distinctive cover at the initial location. Under these conditions, the object may be perceived to pass *through* the background into an indeterminate space beneath the table. Thus, hiding-wells may inadvertently present the infant with a partial *invisible* displacement problem that requires the baby to infer some portion of the object's path of movement. This kind of problem is not usually solved before 18 months (stage V) and the infant typically searches at the first distinctive location. However, when the object merely rests *on* the surface acting as background and all displacements are visible, infants search correctly. This implies that they can identify the object and that the landmark, far from acting as a locus for perseverative responding, structures the immediate visual field in such a way that the infant can directly perceive that a single object has changed its location. Contrary to Piaget, infants can identify an object over a visible change in its spatial position between the ages of eight and 11 months (stage IV), so long as all the necessary spatial information to allow such an inference is available in the baby's visual field.

References

BATTRO, A. M. (Ed.) (1973) *Piaget: Dictionary of Terms*. Oxford: Pergamon Press.

BIRNS, B. (1973) 'Piaget and Wallon: two giants of unequal visibility'. *International Journal of Mental Health*, 1, 24–28.

BOLTON, N. (1978) 'Reflecting on the pre-reflective'. In BURTON, A. and RADFORD, J. (Eds.) *Perspectives on Thinking*. London: Methuen.

BRUNER, J. S. and GARTON, A. (1978) *Human Growth and Development*. Oxford: Oxford University Press.

BRYANT, P. E. (1974) *Perception and Understanding in Young Children*. London: Methuen.

BUTTERWORTH, G. E. (1979) Logical competence in infancy, object percept or object concept? Paper presented to the Society for Research in Child Development, San Francisco.

BUTTERWORTH, G. E. (1978) 'Thought and things: Piaget's theory'. In BURTON, A. and RADFORD, J. (Eds.) *Perspectives on Thinking*. London: Methuen.

BUTTERWORTH, G. E. (1980) 'The origins of auditory-visual perception and visual proprioception in human development'. In PICK, H. and WALK, R. (Eds.) *Perception and Experience*. **Vol. II.** New York: Plenum Press.

BUTTERWORTH, G. E. and CICCHETTI, D. (1978) 'Visual calibration of posture in normal and motor retarded Down's syndrome infants'. *Perception*, 7, 513–525.

BUTTERWORTH, G. E. and COCHRAN, E. (1979) 'What minds have in common is space: a perceptual mechanism for joint reference in infancy'. Paper presented to the Developmental Psychology Section of the British Psychological Society Annual Conference, University of Southampton.

BUTTERWORTH, G. and HICKS, L. (1977) 'Visual proprioception and postural stability in infancy: a developmental study'. *Perception*, 6, 255–262.

DECARIE, T. G. (1965) *Intelligence and Affectivity in Childhood*. New York: International Universities Press.

DENNIS, W. (1972) *Historical Readings in Developmental Psychology*. London: Appleton, Century Crofts.

DONALDSON, M. (1978) *Children's Minds*. Glasgow: Fontana.

ELKIND, D. (1978) *The Child's Reality*. New Jersey: Erlbaum Associates Ltd.

FLAVELL, J. H. (1963) *The Developmental Psychology of Jean Piaget*. London: Van Nostrand.

GIBSON, J. J. (1966) *The Senses Considered as Perceptual Systems*. Boston: Houghton Mifflin.

GUILLAUME, P. (1971) *Imitation in Children*. Chicago: University of Chicago Press. (Translated by E. P. Halperin.)

HAMLYN, D. W. (1978) *Experience and the Growth of Understanding*. London: Routledge and Kegan Paul.

JAMES, W. (1947) *Essays in Radical Empiricism, A Pluralistic Universe*. New York: Longmans, Green and Co. (First published 1912.)

KARMILLOFF-SMITH, A. (1979) *A Functional Approach to Child Language*. Cambridge: Cambridge University Press.

LEE, D. N. and ARONSON, E. (1974) 'Visual proprioceptive control of standing in human infants'. *Perception and Psychophysics*, **15**, 529–532.

MARATOS, O. (1974) 'Origins of Imitation in Early Childhood'. Unpublished Ph.D. thesis, University of Geneva.

MCDOUGALL, W. (1928) *An Outline of Psychology*. 4th Edition. London: Methuen.

MCGARRIGLE, J. and DONALDSON, M. (1974/75) 'Conservation accidents'. *Cognition*, **3**, 307–311.

MELTZOFF, A. and MOORE, M. K. (1977) 'Imitation of facial and manual gestures by human infants'. *Science*, **198**, 75–78.

MOUNOUD, P. and BOWER, T. G. R. (1974) 'Conservation of weight in infants'. *Cognition*, **3**, 29–40.

PHILLIPS, J. L. (1975) *The Origins of Intellect. Piaget's Theory*. 2nd Edition. San Francisco: W. H. Freeman and Co.

PIAGET, J. (1926) *The Language and Thought of the Child*. New York: Harcourt Brace.

PIAGET, J. (1937) 'Principal factors determining intellectual evolution from childhood to adult life'. In *Factors Determining Human Behaviour*. Harvard Tercentenary Publications Cambridge: Harvard University Press.

PIAGET, J. (1951) *Play, Dreams and Imitation in Childhood*. London: Routledge and Kegan Paul.

PIAGET, J. (1953) *The Origin of Intelligence in the Child*. London: Routledge and Kegan Paul.

PIAGET, J. (1954) *The Construction of Reality in the Child*. New York: Basic Books.

PIAGET, J. (1959) *The Language and Thought of the Child*. 3rd Edition. London: Routledge and Kegan Paul.

PIAGET, J. (1962) *Comments on Vygotsky's Critical Remarks Concerning the Language and Thought of the Child and Judgement and Reasoning in the Child*. Boston: MIT Press.

SCAIFE, M. and BRUNER, J. S. (1975) 'The capacity for joint visual attention in the infant'. *Nature*, **253**, 265.

VOYAT, G. (1973) 'The work of Henri Wallon'. *International Journal of Mental Health*, **1**, 4–23.

VYGOTSKY, L. S. (1962) *Thought and Language*. Cambridge, Mass: MIT Press.

WALLON, H. (1973a) 'The psychological development of the child'. *International Journal of Mental Health*, **1**, 29–39.

WALLON, H. (1973b) 'The emotions'. *International Journal of Mental Health*, **1**, 40–52.

WALLON, H. (1973c) 'The origins of thought in the child'. *International Journal of Mental Health*, **1**, 53–66.

WOLFF, P. H. (1960) 'The developmental psychologies of Jean Piaget and psychoanalysis'. *Psychological Issues*, **2**, 1–181.

WOZNIAK, R. H. (1975) 'Dialecticism and structuralism: the philosophical foundation of Soviet psychology and Piagetian congnitive developmental theory'. In RIEGEL, K. F. and ROSENWALD, G. C. (Eds.) *Structure and Transformation: Developmental and Historical Aspects*. **Vol. 3.** New York: John Wiley and Sons.

3

The infant's understanding of space

GAVIN BREMNER

Is the baby born with awareness of the nature of the world around him? Does he know that visual, tactual and auditory images relate to objects situated in an external independent space, or is this the sort of knowledge that he must acquire more or less laboriously during the early stages of development? This is the type of general question that crops up persistently in the study of early cognitive development, and in this chapter I shall summarize some of the theories and findings that may lead us some of the way towards an answer.

Piaget's account of the infants' understanding of space

In view of the title of this book, it is almost inevitable that the starting point for this account should be Piaget's work on the sensorimotor period (Piaget, 1952, 1954), in which the concept of egocentrism occupies a central position. According to Piaget, the infant is born in a state of extreme solipsism, experiencing the world as though it were merely an extension of himself, a series of images contingent on his own actions and devoid of independent material existence. The infant's task during the sensorimotor period is to progress from this initial state to one in which he recognizes the independent existence of the world around him. Not only this, but he must arrive at the conclusion that he is an object in the same way as other objects (physically speaking), situated in a common space and obeying the same spatial rules. In summary, during the first two years, the infant progresses from an initial state of viewing the world as an undifferentiated part of himself, through a period characterized by growing differentiation between self and environment, to a final stage in which a knowing integration is imposed on the differentiation with the end result that he views himself as a part of the environment just like any other object. In effect, he has to get outside himself; first, by realizing that the images experienced within the self arise from objects outside the self, and second, by relinquishing his privileged egocentric viewpoint to realize that his positions and displacements obey the same spatial rules as those of other objects in the environment.

A fundamental part of Piaget's argument is that the development of the concept of space is inextricably linked to the development of the object concept. He claims:

> Space ... is not at all perceived as a container but rather as that which it contains, that is, objects themselves; and if space becomes in any sense a container, it is to the extent that the relationships which constitute the objectification of bodies succeed in becoming intercoordinated until they form a coherent whole (Piaget, 1954, p. 98).

In other words, space is an ordering of objects, so when we talk about space we talk about objects. Later, I shall argue that although this is a valid claim, it may be possible to make a meaningful separation between space and object concepts, particularly during the later stages in their development.

As in the case of the object concept, Piaget (1954) describes six stages in the development of the concept of space. A brief account of this sequence should provide a good background on which to base recent work on infants' spatial knowledge.

In stage I (o to one month) the infant's activities are limited to a number of innate reflexes, such as sucking, rooting, and grasping. On the other hand, during stage II (one to four months) new behaviour patterns emerge that were not present at birth. Piaget claims that during these two stages, space is not in any way differentiated from the actions ventured in it. Action is seen as creating space rather than being situated in space, and displacements of objects are experienced purely as extensions of the subject's own acts. Consequently, the infant fails to distinguish between changes in position and changes in state. Concerning the infant's understanding of depth relations, Piaget (1954) says:

> ... the child certainly perceives at various depths, but there is no indication that he is conscious of these depths or that he groups the perceived displacements on different planes in totalities which are consistent in regard to the objects themselves (p. 111).

During stage III (four to eight months) understanding of space takes a considerable step forward as a result of a new development: The infant begins to observe himself in action, and this coordination of vision and prehension allows the first step to be made towards objectification (and hence externalization) of positions and displacements in space. However, these positions and displacements are not yet interpreted independently of his own activity. Thus the dissociation between self and environment is only beginning. At this stage the infant still does not search for an object hidden under a cover, and Piaget believes that this is further indication that the object's position is only related to the subject and not to other objects, in this case, the cover. During this stage, the infant's understanding of depth relations advances considerably. Through observing his own actions, the zone of space in which activity takes place is externalized and elaborated as a system of relations in depth, albeit relationships between self and objects and not yet between separate objects. On the other hand, regions of space out of reach are not elaborated in this way, taking a similar form to the naïve concept of astronomical space – as if the objects within it were arranged on the inside of a hemisphere bounding the tactual zone, all at the same distance relative to the subject. Despite this limitation, considerable progress has taken place, because during the first two stages space was not externalized at all. Now 'near' space is definitely external. In addition, while retaining the main properties of space during earlier stages, 'distant' space is externalized by virtue of being situated at the boundary of near space.

Stage IV (eight to 12 months) is probably the crucial stage in the sequence for the development of both the concept of space and the object concept. The main feature of this stage is the emergence of search for the hidden object. Apart from its presumed implications for the development of the concept of the permanent object, this newfound ability is seen as a significant factor in the development of understanding of spatial relations. Piaget places emphasis on the fact that in searching for an object hidden under a cover, the infant is coordinating two separate schemes (cover lifting and reaching) in order to obtain the object. This new higher order scheme is specifically suited to obtaining the hidden object and would not have been required as a means of obtaining a visible object. Indeed Piaget notes how the stage III infant will search for an object that is out of sight by virtue of being outside the visual field. In stage III, means-end differentiation emerged, progress over earlier stages in which the activity was the end in itself. This does not qualify as stage IV ability, however, because the same action suffices as when the object is visible. The crucial characteristic of stage IV search is that two separate schemes are combined in an ordered sequence to reach a goal.

The importance of all this from the point of view of spatial development is that according to Piaget, this coordination of separate schemes is accompanied by an understanding of the spatial relationship *between* the objects acted on. In the case of search, the ordering of cover lifting and reaching is accompanied by an understanding of the spatial relationship *between* hidden object and cover, and hence, by realization of the material existence of the object out of sight.

While this constitutes vital progress in the development of the concepts of space and objects, Piaget argues that the infant's thinking retains a considerable subjective element. As evidence for this, he points to a curious search error that stage IV infants make. Whereas the infant has no difficulty in obtaining an object hidden consistently in one place, he runs into considerable difficulties if the object is hidden in a new place. Although he watches the object being hidden there, he shows a strong tendency to search at the original hiding place.

According to Piaget, this indicates the remaining subjective element in the infant's thinking. Although he can relate object and occluder, his capability is limited to a single context, that relating to a particular activity that has been successful in the past. Hence the link between environment and activity is not completely severed. The association between action and object, however, is now one step removed: The object is no longer at the disposal of action (stage III) but at disposal in the *place* where the act has been successful. Hence place is now the middle term. However, Piaget's account leaves us in some doubt as to how *place* is coded at this stage. Is search directed to a place that is the same relative to the subject, or is it directed to a place that is the same relative to the environment? Later on in the chapter I shall review some recent evidence which bears on this sort of question.

During stage IV, the infant becomes better at using his whole body to reach out to more remote objects, and hence the zone of tactual space is progressively expanded, but a poorly elaborated distant space still surrounds the semi-objective near space. Strangely enough, Piaget does not mention crawling as an activity likely to have an effect on the infant's understanding of space, an ability that most infants gain during this stage.

The onset of stage V (12 to 18 months) is marked by the disappearance of the stage IV object-search error. The spatial implication of this is that the infant now views space in an objective manner, as an interrelationship of objects with each other, independent of the subject's activities. The positions of objects can now be represented as well as perceived in their spatial relationships to each other. However, Piaget claims that the infant does not yet understand his own position in space. This seems surprising if we bear in mind the fact that most infants can crawl by the time they enter stage V, and hence have considerable first-hand experience of the consequences of their own displacements. Do they believe that in crawling they bring desired goals *to* them rather than the reverse? Later, I shall present some evidence that challenges Piaget's view on this issue.

Although the infant is capable of representing the positions of objects in an objective manner, he still experiences problems in representing their displacements. If an object is hidden in a box which is then moved under a cover, tipped up to deposit the object, and then returned to its first position, the infant will search in the box but will fail to deduce that the absence of the object there implies its presence under the cover. Failure at this sort of invisible displacement task leads Piaget to believe that the infant is not yet able to represent the object's *displacements* in an objective manner.

During stage VI (18 to 24 months) both of the limitations characteristic of stage V are overcome. The infant solves the invisible displacement problem, evidence that he can represent displacements objectively as well as perceive them thus. In his locomotion, he gains the ability to make detours around obstacles in order to reach goals, which indicates that he can foresee the consequences of his own displacements. Hence he now understands his own positions and displacements in the same way as those of other objects.

This brief summary of Piaget's work cannot have done full justice to his enormously detailed account of sensorimotor development. Nevertheless, I believe that it has picked out the main points in his theory, at any rate in relation to the present topic.

Bower's account

Although Piaget's arguments are often very persuasive, they have not gone un-challenged. The work done by T. G. R. Bower and his colleagues over the past ten years or so has led to an account that differs from Piaget's in some important ways. It is particularly important to include a summary of this alternative position here, because it interprets the infant's difficulties in Piagetian tasks as primarily spatial, rather than related to a limited object concept as such. Probably the main point of disagreement between the two accounts lies in the degree of knowledge of the objective nature of space that each credits to the young infant. In contrast to Piaget's picture of extreme egocentrism in early infancy, Bower's evidence raises the suggestion that the very young infant is much more sophisticated in this respect.

Two areas of Bower's investigations are particularly relevant to the present topic. The first relates to the infant's understanding of depth relations. Bower (1964) found that in an operant conditioning task one- to two-month-old infants were able to maintain a selective response to a cube of a particular size, even when it was presented at various distances and hence presented various retinal image sizes. There was little generalization to cubes of different sizes even if these were presented at such distances as to project the same size of retinal image as the standard at its original distance. This is strong evidence that infants of this age are capable of responding in terms of the distal rather than the proximal stimulus, and, as such, deals a strong blow to Piaget's claim that during the early months objects are perceived purely as images, and depth is not understood. Could it be that the infant compensates distance and retinal image size so as to apply the principle of size constancy *without* understanding the external nature of space at least to the extent of comprehending depth relationships relative to the self? If not, Bower's finding is at considerable odds with Piaget's claim that size constancy is not properly understood until stage IV of the sensorimotor period (eight to 12 months).

The second area, the work of Bower and his colleagues on conceptual development, has given rise to a complex set of results from quite a number of studies. For our purposes a summary of some of the main findings should be adequate. First of all, Bower (1966) argues that the infant appreciates the substantial permanence of the hidden object considerably earlier than Piaget would allow. He found that after watching a stationary object being occluded by a vertical screen, infants as young as two months showed surprise if the object was absent when the screen was removed, a reaction that did not occur in the case of a normal reappearance. From this finding, Bower concluded that at least as early as Piaget's stage II, infants understand the substantial permanence of the hidden object.

This finding is complicated by those arising from subsequent studies of the young infant's tracking abilities (Bower, Broughton and Moore, 1971; Bower and Paterson, 1973); at first sight these tracking results seem at odds with the first finding. If infants had to track an object that passed behind a screen on the middle part of its trajectory, they would continue to track undisturbed if the object stopped behind the screen. More surprisingly, they did the same thing even if the object stopped in full view. Both these findings could have arisen because the infant simply could not arrest the tracking process.

More detailed investigation of tracking records, however, indicated that it was not quite right to say that tracking continued undisturbed. When the object stopped in view, subjects did arrest tracking momentarily, only to resume the same activity a moment later (Bower and Paterson, 1973). From this, Bower and Paterson concluded that the infants did note the presence of the object when it stopped, but that they did not recognize the identity between it and what they had been tracking. Hence they resumed tracking in order to recapture the original object.

In addition to this finding, infants under the age of six months showed no surprise if the object being tracked was exchanged while behind the screen so that a different one emerged at the appropriate moment. On the other hand, they were disturbed if an identical object emerged earlier than it should have done travelling on a uniform trajectory. Bower et al. (1971) conclude that before the age of six months, a moving object is treated more or less as a movement sensation. Its features are not identified and it is dissociated from its stationary self. Hence, when an object moves, it becomes a *different* object. If we accept this conclusion along with the claim that the infant understands the substantial permanence of the stationary object, a curious picture emerges of his understanding of the world. To a large extent he views it in an objective way, as a reality outside himself: Stationary objects are attributed permanence even when out of sight, and depth relationships are understood to the extent necessary for appreciation of size constancy. On the other hand, objects undergo mysterious transformations or annihilations from the baby's point of view whenever they move.

It seems that Bower's description fits in well with the spatial half of Piaget's account. For instance, his claims about the infant's inability to understand the displacements of the object fit in well with Piaget's claim that below stage III the infant fails to differentiate between a change in position and a change in state. On the other hand, unlike Piaget, Bower does credit the young infant with considerable objective knowledge about static objects and space.

Bower et al. (1971) found that by the age of six months, infants overcame their difficulties over object displacements and hence reached an understanding of the identity between moving and stationary objects. So according to this account, by six months they understand objective permanence and spatial displacements. Why, then, do they fail to search for objects in the traditional Piagetian task? Bower claims that this is because they do not understand the relationship between object and cover. The relationship is beyond them, so they assume that the object has been mysteriously replaced by the container, or transformed into the container. Again, it looks as if Bower's position is very much like one half of Piaget's argument without the other: Piaget also claims that understanding of the relationship between object and cover is something that the stage III infant lacks, but he argues that knowledge of this relationship and understanding of continued existence are inseparable; Bower on the other hand, seems to suggest that they are separable.

Bower's position would be hard to accept if we did not note that he is making these claims only about particular types of occlusion: He suggests that the relation 'inside' is more complex than the relation 'behind'. The results of a study by Brown (1973) provide support for this. She found that infants who failed to search in the traditional task (involving the 'inside' relationship) were successful if the object was hidden *behind* a screen. Thus, the argument is that it is only certain complex spatial relationships that the infants fail to comprehend.

This interpretation must be modified slightly in the light of more recent findings. Neilson (*née* Brown, 1977) found that the degree of separation between object and screen was a crucial factor determining whether or not infants would search. If the object-screen separation is very small, infants will not search, whereas if the separation is large, they will search. This result suggests that the problem, at least in this case, has its roots in the *perception* of the relationship rather than in the understanding of it. Could it be a failure to perceive the relationship between object and occluder at the point of disappearance rather than a failure to understand it that leads the infant to conclude that the object has been mysteriously replaced? Maybe it is the small separation between object and occluder rather than the complexity of the relationship that gives the infant problems in the Piagetian task.

One fascinating aspect of Neilson's results was that this separation effect appeared even if the object was placed in full view in front of the screen instead of behind it. Infants did not reach for the object if it was placed directly in front of the screen, whereas they did reach if it was placed some distance in front. Thus, it seems that infants around six months have general difficulties in perceiving or understanding relations between objects that are placed very close together. The simplest interpretation seems to be that if the infant cannot perceive separation between two objects they cannot be treated as separate entities. This sort of suggestion may be useful when we attempt to explain the fact that stage IV infants make search errors even when the object is in plain view (Piaget, 1954; Butterworth, 1977).

Finally, it is interesting to note the similarity between the findings mentioned above and some observations discussed by Piaget (1954), in which stage IV infants failed to reach for an object that had been placed upon another object. Piaget takes this observation as evidence of the limited understanding of object relationships at this stage.

Spatial interpretations of the nine-month-old's search errors

All these results taken together suggest quite strongly that we may have to shift emphasis to spatial factors if we are to understand the infant's problems in classical Piagetian tasks. However, if the spatial problems studied by Bower and Neilson are overcome by the end of stage III (six months) a new spatial problem emerges. Although the stage IV infant knows how to search for a hidden object, whether behind or inside the occluder, he makes spatial errors by searching only in one place even when he has seen the object hidden at a new place. I would argue that this is a phenomenon that requires a *separate* explanation from those presented so far. Although a fragile grasp of the relationship between object and occluder may contribute to the stage IV infant's problems, it is not immediately clear why he should only search at one place as a result. Thus, it seems likely that some other factor, maybe in conjunction with hazy understanding of the relationship between object and occluder, leads to this error.

Before making any suggestions about what this second factor might be, I think it is important to consider some of the recent evidence relating to the stage IV object-search error. Although most of the work in this area has investigated the error for its bearing on the infant's object concept, a number of recent studies have concentrated on a breakdown of the *spatial* factors in the problem, and it is the findings of these studies that I would like to talk about here.

Evans and Gratch (1972) suggested that the stage IV error might be a 'place-going' error that does not really indicate anything about the state of the infant's object concept. They argued that if the error occurred because the infant believed that the object was a 'thing of place A', errors would not be made if the object was switched for a new one on the first occasion of hiding at the new place (B). On the other hand, if it was a simple 'place-going error', changing the object would have no effect on the error-rate. They found no difference in error-rate under these two conditions, subjects making as many errors when a new toy was hidden at the new position as those tested on the standard task, and they took this as support for the 'place-going error' hypothesis. However, it is difficult to see what this result indicates. As Gratch (1975) has since conceded, it is possible that infants in the 'toy change' condition expected to find the old toy at the original position, dissociating from the task the hiding of the new toy.

Doubt is cast on both these interpretations by the results of an attempted replication by Schuberth, Werner and Lipsitt (1978). They noted that in Evans and Gratch's study, subtle procedural differences existed between the groups whether or not the toy was changed before the first 'B' trial. With these differences eliminated, a different pattern of results emerged: Infants in the 'toy change' group made considerably fewer errors than those in the standard task, and Schuberth *et al.* (1978) interpreted this as support for the traditional 'thing of place' explanation. Thus, we have conflicting evidence here: one study supports a simple spatial interpretation of the stage IV error, but there are problems with the interpretation of its results; on the other hand, another study has produced results which support the more traditional interpretation in terms of object concept limitations.

Whether or not the error indicates something about the infant's object concept, we are still faced with the fact that it is a change in position that presents difficulties for the infant. Harris (1973) pointed out that in the standard task a change in the object's position relative to the subject is confounded with a change in the left-right relationship between the hiding and the empty container. The problem here was to establish the relative contribution of these two types of change. Was it only when both happened together that errors occurred, or was a change relative to only one of these frameworks sufficient to cause errors? Furthermore, was it only one framework that was relevant here? Did errors occur when the object's position changed relative to one framework, but not when it changed relative to the other?

Harris' technique for separating self-referent and position-relational changes was ingeniously simple. The infant was seated at a table on which were two hiding positions, one in front of him and the other to his right. After he had found the object at the central position several times, the positions were moved laterally so that the central position was now at the infant's left and the right-hand position was now at his midline. After the change, the object was hidden either in the central position or in the left-hand position. In the first case, the self-referent position of the object remained the same as before, whereas the left-right container relationship was reversed. In the second case, the left-right container relationship remained the same as before whereas the self-referent position of the object was changed.

Harris obtained low error-rates in both these conditions. Unfortunately, however, he did not include a standard task to measure the baseline error-rate under his administration conditions. It seems likely that the low error-rate arose because he did not impose a delay between hiding and search, a factor since shown to be an important determinant of error (Gratch, Appel, Evans, LeCompte and Wright, 1974).

Butterworth (1975) rectified both these problems in his study, but found an additional problem: A low error-rate when the object was hidden at the midline could be due to the fact that the midline position was closer to the infant than the other position. Since this was the sort of result that he obtained in his first study he felt it necessary to conduct a second experiment in which the positions were arranged on a semicircle with the subject as origin, so as to equate their distance from the baby. The results indicated that a change in either the left-right relation or the self-referent code led to errors at much the same level as when both changes took place together. Butterworth concluded that the infant uses both these systems to define the position of the object. Furthermore, he concluded that the stage IV error cannot be explained as a tendency to repeat a successful response, since such a strategy would have led to success whenever the self-referent position of the object remained the same.

At this point it is probably worth recapping a little, just to see how these results are to be interpreted in terms of Piaget's theory and, more specifically, in terms of egocentrism.

First, as I argued a few pages earlier, Piaget claims that the infant's understanding of space and objects is still partially egocentric because the object's position is not yet totally divorced from the actions previously used to find it. However, I pointed out how the object is no longer simply at the disposal of an action as in stage III, but instead is at disposal in the *place* where the action was successful before. This might be taken to mean that action would define spatially the place of search and hence the position would be defined in a self-referent or egocentric manner. I think that there is another possibility, however: namely, that successful action specifies the appropriate place without defining it in spatial terms. Hence, the infant might define positions relative to an external code, but rely egocentrically on past action to specify which of these positions was appropriate. In summary, our problem is to determine whether action has a very strong effect on spatial coding by imposing a self-referent system, or whether its contribution is less specific, simply determining the choice between two positions located within an external framework. Butterworth's evidence that infants do use external relational frameworks lends support to the second interpretation. In any case, whichever interpretation is adopted, the crucial factor determining error seems to be the information that the infant uses to guide search rather than the spatial framework within which he locates the object. After all, if he searched where he saw the object go on 'B' trials, he would be correct no matter what framework he located it in. It is his reliance on out-of-date information (past success at place 'A') which leads to the error.

Whilst on the topic of action, it is worth noting that direct attempts have been made to assess the importance of action in the stage IV task (Landers, 1971; Butterworth, 1974). In both cases, the technique involved running a condition in which the subject was a passive observer during trials at the first position. The object was hidden and revealed several times without the infant being allowed to search. Despite this limited experience, roughly the same number of infants as usual made an error when they were allowed to search on the first 'B' trial. Although these results allow us to conclude that overt manual action is not a necessary condition for error, I think we must bear in mind that Piaget observed this sort of error in the infant's looking habits as well as in search. It may be that in the 'passive' conditions above, eye movements took over the role normally performed by manual action. Nevertheless, such an interpretation is of interest because it suggests that if action has any effect on the direction of search, it is really at quite an abstract level. In addition, the presence of the error in looking habits lends support to the idea that if we adopt Piaget's standpoint a spatial analysis of the stage IV error must be divided into two components: one relating to understanding of the object-occluder relationship through coordination of two manual action schemes, and another relating to the perseverative error itself, which occurs when coordination of schemes is not part of the task.

Second, how does all this relate to egocentrism? From Piaget's point of view it is the continuing link between action and external world that marks the infant's behaviour as egocentric. I have argued that Piaget's writings are rather vague over the details of this action-environment link during stage IV, and it seems that all the evidence points to the nine-month-old infant being less egocentric than the stronger interpretation of Piaget's theory would have us believe. In addition, I have suggested that the infant's egocentrism, as reflected by the error, may not bear any clear relation to the type of spatial code that he adopts. For this reason I have avoided talking of an *egocentric* spatial code, using the term 'self-referent' instead. Although the type of egocentrism characterized by some degree of failure to differentiate between self and environment might lead to use of the self-referent spatial code, the two are really quite different notions. Whereas it seems essential that Piaget's type of egocentrism must wane (if it is present in the first place), the self-referent code is still useful to us as adults. Hence, in the latter case we want to know how the code becomes restricted to appropriate cases, rather than how it vanishes completely.

Spatial frameworks used by infants

Clearly, the account is becoming complicated, and in the light of the evidence it seems that we are not much closer to an explanation of the stage IV error. Certainly, there are various reasons why it is difficult to decide what this behaviour indicates about the infant's object concept. Since, in this chapter, the emphasis is on spatial understanding, I have not dwelt on interpretations in terms of the object concept, but sufficient indication of the problem is given by noting the possibility that the infant searches, not because he knows that the object is under the cover, but because he believes that action at a particular place recreates the object (an argument that Piaget would use to explain the behaviour of the stage III infant but not the behaviour of the stage IV infant).

On the other hand, spatial interpretation of the error does seem to have begun to bear fruit (Harris, 1973; Butterworth, 1975). I believe we may be able to gain more information about the infant's ideas about positions in space from this phenomenon, particularly if we attempt to draw a clear distinction between two questions:

(1) Why does the stage IV infant treat only one position as the appropriate place for search?
(2) Given that he is likely to search at only one place, how does he define that place spatially?

At present, most of the arguments relevant to the first question have been related to the object concept, and we do not seem to be close to an answer. I shall present an alternative explanation of the phenomenon which is based on the functional characteristics of places rather than on the physical nature of objects and space. Before doing so, however, I shall describe some experiments performed as an attempt to reach an answer to the second question.

Butterworth's (1975) evidence suggests that the answer to the second question may be quite complex, with the infant relying on the self-referent code and the relationship between containers in deciding where to search. In addition, we felt that there was another confounding factor in both the standard stage IV task and the modified versions used by both Harris and Butterworth: Any change in the object's position relative to the infant is accompanied by a change in its position relative to stable features of the environment (for instance, the table), since the infant stays in the same place throughout the task. Our question was whether the infant errs by responding to the same place relative to himself, or whether he errs by repeating a response to the same place relative to some feature or features of the environment outside the immediate container relationship. We used a fairly simple technique to separate these two factors (Bremner and Bryant, 1977). After five 'A' trials the infant was moved round to the opposite side of the table, and the object was hidden again with the infant watching from his new position. In the case of one group (A) the object was hidden in the opposite position from before, whereas in the case of the other group (B) it was hidden in the same position as before (see Figure 1). In order to provide external spatial cues, the table was painted so that one side was white and the other was black. If infants responded to the same self-referent position as before, those in Group A would be correct whereas those in Group B would make errors. On the other hand, if they responded to the same position relative to environment cues (for instance, the spatial ones which we provided), those in Group A would make errors and those in Group B would be correct.

The results were quite clear. Very few infants in Group A made an error on the first trial after the rotation, whereas most of the infants in Group B did err. We can summarize these results by saying that after the rotation there was a clear tendency for infants to change the side of the table at which they searched, but no evidence that they changed their response. These results were backed up from two other conditions in which we rotated the table instead of the infant. Again, the same

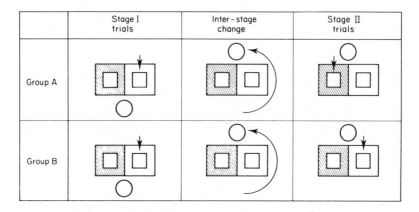

Fig. 1   The crucial conditions from Bremner and Bryant's experiment

results emerged. Few subjects erred when the object was hidden at the same self-referent position as before although this involved reaching at a position on a different background, and a large number of errors occurred when the object was hidden on the same background but at the opposite position relative to the infant.

Taken as a whole, these results suggest that most infants were defining the position of search relative to themselves. Whether this was a case of response repetition, or the result of self-referent definition of position at the cognitive level is not clear. However, there was certainly no evidence that infants were using cues contained in the table or the rest of the environment to guide their search.

Nevertheless, I was not convinced that this was the whole story. Although we had differentiated the sides of the table in this experiment in order to provide external spatial cues for the infant, it seemed possible that these cues were not adequate, and that in the presence of more salient cues, infants might respond differently. With this in mind, I performed a similar experiment (Bremner, 1978a) in which the cues were enhanced by exchanging the black and white table and grey covers for a grey table with a black and a white cover. I hoped that cover differentiation would provide a more salient spatial cue than background differentiation.

This simple alteration produced a dramatic change in infants' performance in condition B. In this case only a small number of infants made an error, a significant improvement over the background cue case. In Group A, infants performed at much the same level as previously, although this involved lifting a differently coloured cover after the transformation. Thus, it seems safe to conclude that success in Group B was not simply the result of responding to a particular cover

53

rather than searching for the object. It seems that the infant is capable of defining the position of search relative to external cues, but only if these cues are sufficiently strong.

The story is not so simple, however, since it turned out that these cover cues did not have such a strong effect in the equivalent condition in which the transformation involved reversal of the cues instead of rotation of the infant. In this condition, the improvement was only slight and certainly was not significant. Thus, it seemed that provision of stronger cues was not sufficient on its own to lead to a shift from self-referent to external coding. A movement of the infant was also necessary, maybe because it served some sort of prompting function. The suggestion here is that we must provide external cues *and* prompt the infant to use them if we are to see him rely on them, and movement of the infant may serve this function by altering him to a change in the task. This is a possibility that I shall expand on later.

Unfortunately, there is one problem in interpreting the data presented so far. The assumption has been that most infants were searching at the same place (however defined) both before and after the transformation, and that when infants were successful after the transformation this was because the addition of strong cues had made them change their coding of the 'same place' from self-referent to external-referent. That is, the experimental manipulation did not lead to the removal of the error, only to the re-definition of the one place at which they searched. There is another possibility, however. The infant-movement condition may simply have led to non-perseveration. Maybe his movement plus the presence of strong cues led the infant to search where he saw the object go on post-transformation trials, rather than where he had found it before. It is difficult to see why this should happen only in the presence of strong cues. This sort of explanation remains a possibility, but although it does not invalidate the main findings about the infant's understanding of space it makes detailed interpretation of the results difficult.

At this point, I was beginning to have reservations about the usefulness of the stage IV task as a tool for finding out about the infant's understanding of space. What was required was a task that would eliminate the problem of deciding whether success resulted from perseveration to an external cue or from reliance on post-transformation experience, but at the same time I wanted to retain the useful features of the old task. The obvious solution seemed to be to hide the object but not allow the infant to search until he had been moved to the opposite side of the table (or until the table had been rotated). This would eliminate any additional information after the transformation which the infant might have used in the old task.

Very similar results emerged when this new task was presented to nine-month-olds (Bremner, 1978b). When cover cues were used, infants were very good at finding an object that had been hidden before they moved, but were less successful if background differentiation cues were used instead (only about half were successful). The same cue effect appeared in conditions in which the table was rotated instead of the infant, but under these conditions performance was worse overall. The majority of subjects made an error when background cues were used whereas roughly half made an error when cover cues were used. Thus, the same two effects emerged from this study as well, if anything more clearly. The first is a simple effect: Stronger cues enhanced performance. The second effect is not so easily explained and is certainly more interesting: Infants performed better at the new spatial transformation task when the transformation involved movement of themselves rather than movement of the array.

Of course, there is an alternative explanation of the movement effect: Instead of superior performance being the result of moving the infant between stages, it could have arisen because the object remains stable relative to the environment as a whole in the 'infant movement' case but not in the 'array movement' case. Thus, we could argue that the effect indicates that the infant can search successfully in this sort of task as long as the object's position stays stable relative to the whole environment and not just to the immediate cues. If this were the case, however, we would have difficulty explaining the absence of a difference between subject- and array-movement conditions in the first study (Bremner and Bryant, 1977). If the less immediate environment was used as referent then one would expect object stability to have a stronger effect when the immediate cues were less strong, rather than the reverse. Thus, the idea that movement of the subject serves some sort of prompting function seems by far the simplest explanation of the data.

The movement effect suggests that infants are better at taking account of the consequences of their own movements than of movements of objects. Whether or not this happens because their own movement prompts them to a change in the task more than a movement of the array, the result runs counter to Piaget's claim that the infant does not arrive at an understanding of his own displacements until late in the sensorimotor stage. Hence, his theory may require modification in this respect.

The results I have mentioned are somewhat limited because they are gathered from only one age-group. However, one study using a formally similar task has been performed, this time with subjects tested at three different ages (Acredolo, 1978). In this case, only a 'subject rotation' task was presented. Infants were placed in a small rectangular room with windows to their left and right. They were trained to anticipate the appearance of an experimenter who appeared at the same window each time, the cue being the sound of a centrally-placed buzzer. After this response had been established, subjects were rotated through 180° about the mid-point of the room, so that the window that had been to their left was now to their right, and *vice versa*. The crucial part of the experiment was observing the direction of the infant's response when the buzzer sounded after this movement.

Acredolo presented this task both with and without spatial cues. In the 'landmark condition' the correct window was surrounded by a large star, whereas, in the other condition no specific cues were provided. Subjects were tested at six, 11 and 16 months under one or other of these conditions. The results were as follows. At six months, the majority of infants responded to the same side of themselves after they had been moved, and thus anticipated the event at the wrong window. This happened under both conditions, so the landmark did not seem to have any effect at this age. On the other hand, at 11 months, although performance was still bad in the 'no landmark' condition, only half of the 'landmark' group made an error after rotation. Thus, at this age, infants seem to derive some benefit from provision of a spatial cue in this task. However, the only clear change in performance took place between 11 and 16 months, with the majority in 16-month-olds performing correctly from their new position whether or not a spatial cue was provided.

These results suggest that strong spatial cues may be really important only while the infant is acquiring the ability to use external frames of reference, and the age-related change in ability complements the findings with nine-month-olds fairly well.

It may be that the simplest interpretation of some of the more puzzling results reported above relates to the infant's general spatial experience around the age of nine months. I shall argue that initially the infant is likely to find a self-referent spatial strategy fairly adequate in his dealings with the world, but that later, and in particular when he begins to crawl, such a strategy will become very much less successful.

The essential factor in the argument is that the immobile infant is limited to positions in his environment that his parents select for him, and that in many of these habitual positions he will be placed in a consistent orientation. A clearer way of putting this might be to say that the infant is presented with a relatively small number of different views of the world that are inseparable from the context in which they arise (examples of particular contexts might be, lying in his cot, having his nappy changed, etc.). Within a particular context, stable objects, and even his parents, are likely to appear in consistent positions relative to himself. Of course, there are likely to be some cases in which the same object can be seen from more than one of his habitual positions and this is clearly true of two objects, his parents. Nevertheless, the suggestion here is that context is a strong determinant of where he will look for an object. For example, when placed in his cot he will be successful in finding his mobile by fixating the same self-referent position each time, whereas while having his nappy changed he may find the same mobile while fixating a different self-referent position. The important idea is that the context in which he finds himself determines where he looks, and the fact that he succeeds in finding the same object from different positions does not necessarily indicate a proper understanding of space, or indeed the realization that it is the same object that he sees in both cases.

Even when the infant grows out of this contextual dependence in the case of visible objects, the same limitation might well restrict his judgement as far as cases of disappearance and reappearance are concerned. His parents will disappear and reappear at particular places, and toys are likely to be found in the same box (maybe in a slightly mysterious way because it is rarely the infant who puts them there).

The importance of this argument is its prediction that up to a certain age the infant will search for objects at a location defined relative to himself, but that when he becomes mobile he is likely to find this strategy less satisfactory. As a result of his new mobility he will find himself in many more positions and orientations than before. The context will no longer determine his position. In order to cope with the large number of new perspectives with which he is faced, he will have to develop a way of linking them. The obvious way of doing this would be to relate positions to a stable external framework instead of to the unstable self.

It should be noted that this increase in perspectives may well occur before the infant begins to crawl, as a result of changes in the way the infant's parents treat him as he gets older. Initially, he may be limited to perhaps three or four positions, for instance, in his cot, having his nappy changed, being fed or played with on a parent's knee. Later, and particularly when he is able to sit upright, he is likely to be given more freedom of position while he is awake, being placed in a number of positions on the floor and in chairs. Thus, although the onset of crawling is likely to produce the major increase in perspectives, other factors will also contribute to this.

One important suggestion arising from all this is that around the time that the infant is beginning to find the self-referent strategy unsatisfactory, he may be aware that it is particularly in the cases when he has just been moved that some other strategy is required. This would explain the good performance of infants in the 'infant movement' conditions of my experiments (Bremner, 1978a and b).

Can we also arrive at a possible explanation of the stage IV error by looking at the information that the infant may gain from his environment around this time? It may be that before he has a full understanding of relationships between objects, he makes certain simplifying assumptions about the places where hidden objects are to be found. Although the young infant often removes objects from containers (e.g. his toy box) he is not so often the one who puts them back. Thus, when he has an expectation about the location of an object this may have been gained more from finding it than from seeing it hidden there. It is possible to form a tentative explanation of the stage IV error based on this assumption. On the first 'A' trial the infant searches where he sees the object disappear, because he has no prior hypothesis about where it should be found. When he finds it, however, this experience establishes that particular place as the place where the object is to be found, and henceforth the strategy of searching at this 'appropriate place' dominates the strategy of searching where he sees the object go. Thus, when the object is hidden in a new position, he makes an error.

All this may leave the reader in doubt as to why the infant should rely on his idea about the 'appropriate place' for search, even when he has just seen the object hidden at some other place. This sort of behaviour would seem more likely if the habit of specifying an appropriate place for search is interpreted as a way of making simplifying assumptions about his world in order to understand it. Maybe in order to make sense of the world, he has to make simplifying generalizations about the nature of events. Thus he may rely heavily on these general rules when reliance on perception might be more fruitful but more of a strain on his understanding. This seems very similar to the type of processes that adults indulge in all the time, except that the infant's simplifying generalizations are probably more gross.

Conclusion

What can we say in conclusion about egocentrism? Most of the recent evidence, particularly the work of T. G. R. Bower and his colleagues, suggests that the infant is not as egocentric as Piaget suggested. Furthermore, the work on spatial coding (Acredolo, 1978; Bremner, 1978a and b) indicates that under appropriate cueing conditions, the nine-month-old infant is capable of relying on external codes, and that 16-month-olds are capable of doing this even when strong cues are not provided. Although it is not clear that this evidence runs counter to Piaget's position, it is support for the view that the infant has considerable awareness of the world around him. In addition, the nine-month-old's awareness of the consequences of his own movements in rotation tasks (Bremner, 1978a and b) goes against Piaget's claim that this ability is only gained at the end of the sensorimotor period. Finally, I outlined a very tentative explanation of the infant's spatial errors based on the idea that limitations of his *experience* may determine the strategies that he employs. Rather than being a direct function of his cognitive abilities (or limitations), such strategies may often result from external constraints on his experience. Whether or not we believe that the infant is egocentric, we still have the problem of establishing the degree to which constraints on his experience of the world lead to limitations in his spatial ability.

References

ACREDOLO, L. P. (1978) 'Development of spatial orientation in infancy'. *Developmental Psychology*, **14**, 224–234.
BOWER, T. G. R. (1964) 'Discrimination of depth in premotor infants'. *Psychonomic Science*, **1**, 368.
BOWER, T. G. R. (1966) 'Object permanence and short-term memory in the human infant'. Unpublished manuscript, University of Edinburgh.

BOWER, T. G. R., BROUGHTON, J. M. and MOORE, M. K. (1971) 'Development of the object concept as manifested in changes in the tracking behavior of infants between 7 and 20 weeks'. *Journal of Experimental Child Psychology*, **11**, 182–193.

BOWER, T. G. R. and PATERSON, J. G. (1973) 'The separation of place, movement, and object in the world of the infant'. *Journal of Experimental Child Psychology*, **15**, 161–168.

BREMNER, J. G. (1978a) 'Spatial errors made by infants: inadequate spatial cues or evidence of egocentrism?' *British Journal of Psychology*, **69**, 77–84.

BREMNER, J. G. (1978b) 'Egocentric versus allocentric spatial coding in nine-month-old infants: factors influencing the choice of code'. *Developmental Psychology*, **14**, 346–355.

BREMNER, J. G. and BRYANT, P. E. (1977) 'Place versus response as the basis of spatial errors made by young infants'. *Journal of Experimental Child Psychology*, **23**, 162–171.

BROWN, I. (1973) 'A Study of Object Permanence'. Unpublished honours thesis, University of Edinburgh.

BUTTERWORTH, G. (1974) 'The Development of the Object Concept in Human Infants'. Unpublished D.Phil. thesis, University of Oxford.

BUTTERWORTH, G. (1975) 'Object identity in infancy: the interaction of spatial location codes in determining search errors'. *Child Development*, **46**, 866–870.

BUTTERWORTH, G. (1977) 'Object disappearance and error in Piaget's stage IV task'. *Journal of Experimental Child Psychology*, **23**, 391–401.

EVANS, W. F. and GRATCH, G. (1972) 'The stage IV error in Piaget's theory of object concept development: difficulties in object conceptualisation or spatial location?' *Child Development*, **43**, 682–688.

GRATCH, G. (1975) 'Recent studies based on Piaget's view of object concept development'. In Cohen & Salapatek (Eds.) *Infant Perception: From Sensation to Cognition*, **Vol. II**, New York: Academic Press.

GRATCH, G., APPEL, K. J., EVANS, W. F., LECOMPTE, G. K. and WRIGHT, N. A. (1974) 'Piaget's stage IV object concept error: evidence of forgetting or object conception?' *Child Development*, **45**, 71–77.

HARRIS, P. L. (1973) 'Perseverative errors in search by young infants'. *Child Development*, **44**, 28–33.

LANDERS, W. F. (1971) 'The effect of differential experience on infants' performance in a Piagetian stage IV object-concept task'. *Developmental Psychology*, **5**, 48–54.

NEILSON, I. E. (1977) 'A Reinterpretation of the Development of the Object Concept in Infancy'. Unpublished Ph.D. thesis, University of Edinburgh.

PIAGET, J. (1952) *The Origins of Intelligence in Children*. New York: Basic Books.

PIAGET, J. (1954) *The Construction of Reality in the Child*. New York: Basic Books.

SCHUBERTH, R. E., WERNER, J. S. and LIPSITT, L. P. (1978) 'The stage IV error in Piaget's theory of object concept development: a reconsideration of the spatial localization hypothesis'. *Child Development*, **49**, 744–748.

4

Visual perspective-taking in children

M. V. COX

Introduction

Whereas the previous chapter dealt with the *infant's* understanding of space, the present chapter is mainly concerned with the *child's* understanding. Piaget's claim that the young child's basic egocentrism explains his failure to appreciate another person's point of view in a perspective-taking task will be examined.

Perspective-taking involves the ability to consider another person's view. Kurdek and Rodgon (1975) point out that this is a cognitive skill with a multi-dimensional nature. The three dimensions of perspective-taking are:

(1) *perceptual* perspective-taking, the ability to assume another person's perceptual viewpoint;
(2) *cognitive* perspective-taking, the ability to assess another person's knowledge; and,
(3) *affective* perspective-taking, the ability to assess another person's emotional state.

In this chapter I shall be dealing with the first kind of perspective-taking, viz. perceptual, sometimes referred to as visual or spatial.

A person's view of the world will change as he moves about: the apparent size and shape of objects will alter as well as their position relative to other objects and to the person himself. The world does not remain static, however; objects (including people) also move or are moved so that a person's view may change even while he remains stationary. Although it would be possible for the observer and other objects to move in synchrony so as to maintain a constant view, normally observer and objects move out of synchrony so that the observer's view changes. Perspective ability involves this knowledge about others' changing views as well as one's own: since two people do not normally occupy the same position in space, their views will be different.

In the literature a distinction is made between two types of observer-object relations. In one, called *perspectives problems*, the subject is asked to predict what a stationary array would look like from a different position. In the other, called *rotation problems*, the subject is asked to predict the view of an object if it were rotated (generally, towards himself) while he himself remains stationary. Huttenlocher and Presson (1973) and Strauss and Cohen (1974) have shown that a perspectives task is more difficult than a rotation task. Furthermore, from an analysis of the types of errors made for each task, they have suggested that one task is not simply the reverse of the other (i.e. the subject imagines himself rotated around a stationary object-array *versus* the stationary subject imagines the object-array rotated), but a different sort of task. A problem here is that, in the rotation task, the subject was asked to imagine his *own* view of a rotated object whereas, in the perspectives task, he was asked to imagine *another* observer's view rather than his own. So it is not clear whether the difficulty in performance was due to the nature of the perspectives task *per se*, or whether it was a difficulty in imagining another observer's view rather than one's own from a new position.

Harris and Bassett (1976), however, have conducted a similar experiment in which the subject was asked to imagine his own view in both a rotation and a perspectives task. Six-year-olds found the perspectives task significantly harder than the rotation task. Thus, using a more tightly-controlled experiment, the original results of Huttenlocher and Presson (1973) were confirmed.

In their research, Piaget and Inhelder (1956, 1970) used both perspectives and rotation problems (rotation problems were solved by seven or eight years of age whereas perspectives problems were not solved until nine or ten years) but did not make a direct comparison between them. Nevertheless, it is assumed that Piaget and Inhelder regard the underlying processes as similar.

Piaget's method

The best known study of the development of perspective-taking is that of Piaget and Inhelder (1956). They asked children to imagine what apparent shape an object, such as a needle or a thin metal disc, would present when viewed from different positions.

Immediately at least two problems arose. How does one get the child to understand that the task involves the *apparent* shape and not the *actual* shape of the object? And how can one find out how a child *imagines* the shape?

The first problem was solved, according to Piaget and Inhelder, by introducing a small doll who viewed the same object at right-angles to the child. Thus, a needle seen end-on to the child would appear full-length from the doll's position.

This method was supplemented with one in which the object was rotated in front of the child and he was asked to predict the apparent shapes resulting from further similar changes. (See Figure 1.)

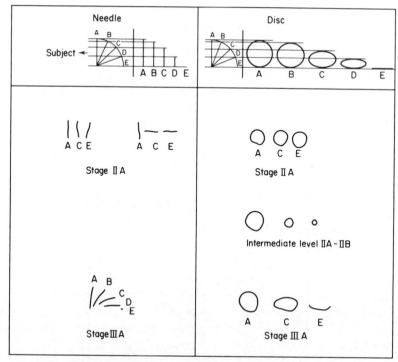

Fig. 1 Examples of children's attempts to represent successive presentations of the needle and the disc, seen in perspective (Piaget and Inhelder, 1956)

The second problem, that of finding out how a child *imagines* the shape, was also solved by using two techniques. First, the child made a drawing. To counteract possible deficiencies in motor skills, the second method involved asking the child to choose a shape from a selection of drawings; these included the errors frequently found in children's spontaneous drawings.

The more famous task that Piaget and Inhelder used in their study of perspective-taking is the 'three-mountains' task. This was used to study the child's representation of a *group* of objects seen from different viewpoints. The mountains were made of *papier mâché* and were placed on a one metre square base. As seen from position A the largest mountain was at the back of the display; it was grey with a snow-cap. A brown mountain was to the left, displaying a red cross on its summit. In the right-foreground was a green mountain surmounted by a small house. There was a zigzag path down the side of the green mountain when viewed from position C and a rivulet descending the brown mountain when viewed from B. The only information given about exact sizes is that the heights of the mountains varied from 12 to 30 cm. (See Figure 2.)

63

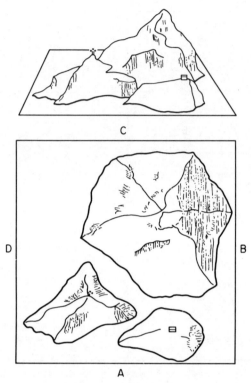

Fig. 2 Three-mountains model used by Piaget and Inhelder (1956)

The child was asked to represent the view of the mountains from his own position at A. Then a wooden doll (about two to three cm. high) was put at position C and the child was asked to represent the view that could be seen from there. This procedure was repeated for positions B and D. The child was then asked to move to position B (or C or D) and to represent the view from there; in addition he was asked to represent the view from A or other positions he had already occupied.

Piaget and Inhelder elicited three different modes of response. First, the child was asked to reproduce the doll's view by arranging three pieces of cardboard shaped like the mountains. Second, the child was asked to select the doll's view from a set of ten pictures (each measuring 20 by 28 cm.). In the third task, the child was asked to choose one picture and then decide which position the doll must occupy to have that particular view of the mountains.

Piaget's stages and explanation

Piaget and Inhelder do not give any details of the subjects they used for the one-object-array task, but, in a rare example, they do give more details in the three-mountains task. In fact, 100 children were used: 21 between 4 and 6; 6 years, 30 between 6; 7 and 8 years, 33 between 8 and 9; 6 years, and 16 between 9; 6 and 12 years.

Piaget and Inhelder interpreted the children's responses as falling into a series of stages of perspective ability – the results of both the one-object-array and the three-mountains task revealing the same stages:

Stage I   (below 4 years). The child does not understand the meaning of the questions put to him. Piaget and Inhelder conclude that it is pointless to attempt any consistent studies or to report the answers given.

Stage IIA   (4 to 5; 6 years). The child does not distinguish between his own and the doll's view of the object(s). In the one-object task, he shows the shape of the object as the same whatever its position relative to the observer. He represents the object in a typical or stereotypical way regardless of the *apparent* shape he sees (see Figure 1). In the three-mountains task, also, the child shows the mountains from a single point of view, that of his own. What he actually sees is adopted as the typical, stereotyped view of the mountains. As Fer (p. 219) says, '*That* [his own view] *is the right one; he sees the three mountains just as they are* (!)' The child at this stage is regarded as egocentric, i.e. he centres his perception on his own viewpoint although he fails to realize that it is his own viewpoint.

Stage IIB   (5; 6 to 7 years). At this stage there are the first signs of discrimination between viewpoints. The child becomes aware of the distinctions between different views of an object and of the changing relationships among objects according to the particular point of view. However, he does not know how to effect these changes and is unsuccessful in his attempts.

Stage IIIA   (7 or 7; 6 to 8; 6 or 9 years). The child draws a clear distinction between different points of view but has not yet developed a fully-organized system of correspondence between viewpoint and view. In the one-object array, for instance, the child portrays the qualitative change of a shift in viewpoint, but does not understand that these are linked in a continuous, quantitative fashion (see Figure 1). In the three-mountains task, the child understands how some of the relationships (e.g. before–behind, left–right) among the mountains vary with changing points of view, but he does not consider these relationships simultaneously.

Stage IIIB   (8 ; 6 or 9 +). The child develops a comprehensive operational system for dealing with perspective changes. In distinguishing between successive views of a single object, the child is no longer content with mere qualitative seriation, but quantifies these successive differences. In the three-mountains case, changes among the relationships of the mountains arc considered simultaneously within an overall framework.

The problem of egocentrism

The stage II child's lack of success in a perspectives task is attributed by Piaget and Inhelder to his egocentrism which is regarded as a fundamental trait of the preoperational child's thinking. Typically, he reproduces or chooses his own view and attributes it to another observer. He 'appears to be rooted to his own viewpoint in the narrowest and most restricted fashion so that he cannot imagine any perspective but his own' (Piaget and Inhelder, 1956, p. 242). The child does not realize, however, that he is responding with his own view. His egocentrism is therefore unconscious. Eventually, 'consciousness of the egocentrism destroys egocentrism' (Piaget, 1959, p. 268).

It is not at all clear what Piaget means by 'egocentrism' and the term has created a good deal of confusion. Braine (1962, p. 42) has said of Piaget, 'Instead of specifying his constructs in terms of evidence, he illustrates them with a wealth of suggestive observation.' Piaget himself has said of egocentrism, 'That term has had the worst interpretation of any word I have used' (in Hall, 1970, p. 28); this is not surprising as his writings on the subject are rather confusing and often appear to be contradictory. It is not easy to assess whether the difficulty results from a lack of clarity of exposition or from an undeveloped notion. It is not immediately clear, for instance, whether the child is supposed *not* to know that views other than his present one are possible, whether he knows that his own movement will result in a change of view but that he has no knowledge of the visual percepts of others, whether he knows that his own view can change but others see the same changing view as he does, or whether he knows that others may see a different view from himself but he lacks the skills for predicting these views.

Some of these issues can be clarified by referring to Piaget and Inhelder's original writing. They say that the young child is 'already perfectly well aware that the appearance of the group of mountains changes together with the observer's point of view' (p. 216). (The 'observer' here refers to the child himself.) This should not be surprising since, from their second year, babies can turn objects round or turn their heads or bodies in order to get different views. Of course, Piaget regards these changes as *successive perceptions* rather than anticipatory, *imagined* changes. Nevertheless, in the same way, the young child in the three-mountains experiment, is not 'surprised to find that in moving from position A to position C opposite, he has to make a new picture quite different from the previous one' (p. 217). So, he does realize that different views are possible.

Shantz and Watson (1970) also found that the young child expects to see a different view when he moves to a new position. In their experiment, the child first viewed a scene (indoor scene: doll seated in a chair in front of a television; outdoor scene: a house, a car, and a tree with a road and footpath) through a slot in the top of a box. He then moved round to the opposite side of the box and viewed the scene again. In the 'real' condition the scene inside the box remained stationary, but in the trick condition the scene was rotated by a hidden pulley system (through either 180° or 90°). When the scene was rotated through 180° and the child also moved through 180° he was confronted by his original view. Shantz and Watson concluded that about half the sample of 48 three- to five-year-olds noticed the difference between the real and the trick conditions as judged by their verbalizations (expressing surprise, amusement, or perplexity). Furthermore, 14 subjects also attributed the view in the trick condition to a rotation of the scene inside the box. There was also a significant effect when frequency of facial responses indicating surprise or perplexity was recorded.

In the three-mountains task, Piaget and Inhelder report that when the child moves to a new position not only can he construct his new view of the mountains but he can also *reconstruct* the view seen from his original position, thus demonstrating that he can imagine different views. What he lacks, however, is a mobile concept of the transformation which will occur in a view which he has *not yet* seen. In other words although the very young child can represent present views and past views he cannot *anticipate* new views. Thus he is 'centred exclusively on his own viewpoint' (Piaget and Inhelder, 1956, p. 218). Eiser's work (1974) adds further support to this argument. She compared the performance of a group of six- to eight-year-olds who were allowed to walk round the model mountains before predicting views from different positions (recognition condition) with a group who predicted the different views without having seen them before (inference condition). Children in the inference condition made significantly more own-view errors (i.e. they chose their own view and attributed it to the other observer who was positioned either opposite or at right angles to the child) than those in the recognition condition.

Although the studies discussed so far show that the young child does expect his own view to change when he moves to a new position and that he can reconstruct views already seen, they do not tell us anything about the child's knowledge of other people's views. In other words, the child's difficulty in a perspectives task may not be in realizing that his own view changes but in knowing that others have visual percepts and that these are independent of his own. Piaget and Inhelder (1956) maintain that although the preoperational child is perfectly well aware that the appearance of objects changes with his own point of view (p. 216) he is 'quite unaware that he possesses a viewpoint distinct from those of other observers' (p. 243).

The growth of the child's knowledge concerning the visual percepts of others has been the subject of study by Flavell and his colleagues.

Masangkay, McCluskey, McIntyre, Sims-Knight, Vaughn, and Flavell (1974) presented $2\frac{1}{2}$- and 3-year-olds with a picture task and an eye-position task. In the picture task a piece of card was positioned vertically between the child and the experimenter so each had a certain specific view – e.g. a picture of a dog for one and a picture of a cat for the other. The child was asked to state what *he* could see and what the experimenter could see. In the eye-position task the child was required to specify which of four toys the experimenter was looking at. Most children were successful in both tasks.

Lempers, Flavell, and Flavell (1977) used subjects from four age-groups: 1-year-olds, $1\frac{1}{2}$-year-olds, 2-year-olds, and $2\frac{1}{2}$-year-olds. These children were observed in their own homes in a series of tasks. Ten tasks were called 'percept production tasks'. Each child was asked to show an object to an observer (usually his mother). In one task, for instance, a photograph of a familiar object was glued to the inside bottom surface of a hollow cube and the child was asked to show the picture to the observer. A further four tasks were called 'percept deprivation tasks': for instance, in one task, the child was required to hide a toy car from the observer by moving it behind a screen. Two more tasks were called 'percept diagnosis tasks': the child was asked to state which object the observer was looking at.

It is interesting that whereas the two-year-olds moved objects in an adult way – i.e. by turning the object toward the observer with the result that the child himself could no longer see it – the $1\frac{1}{2}$-year-olds when showing the object tried to keep it visible to both themselves and the other observer. Purely 'egocentric' responding – i.e., positioning the object so it was visible to the child himself but not to another – was virtually non-existent. Nearly all of the two-year-olds understood the need for the observer actually to look at the object: 11 out of 12 two-year-olds moved the observer's hands away from her eyes in order to show her the object. It seemed necessary for the two-year-olds to establish visual contact with the observer before showing her something; showing something to an unseen observer proved to be a very difficult task. Successful showing responses preceded hiding, presumably because in hiding it is necessarily the case that the object is not visible to at least one of the observers.

In a subsequent study, Flavell, Shipstead, and Croft (1978) investigated young children's understanding of object hiding. They found that $2\frac{1}{2}$- to $3\frac{1}{2}$-year-olds could nonegocentrically hide an object by placing it on the opposite side of a screen from another person and yet visible to themselves. Similarly, Hughes (cited by Donaldson, 1978) found that 3¾-year-olds achieved a success-rate of 88 % in a hiding game: each child was asked to hide a boy doll from two toy policemen positioned at separate points of two intersecting 'walls'. (See Figure 3.)

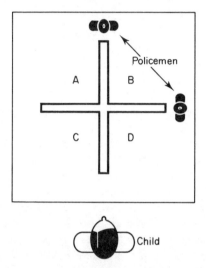

Fig. 3   Apparatus used in the Hughes study (Donaldson, M. *Children's Minds*, p. 22)

So, what do these results tell us? They suggest that young children (by three years old at least) realize that other people have visual percepts and that they will take steps to manipulate objects (or, if necessary, the observer herself) so that an observer can see them; furthermore, they suggest that young children understand that others may see objects which they themselves do not see, and *vice versa*.

To summarize the issues so far: in addition to the work of Piaget and Inhelder and Shantz and Watson which showed that the young child expects his own view to change as he moves position, the work of Flavell and his colleagues shows that the very young child also has expectations about the visual percepts of others. In what way then can children be described as 'egocentric'? A feasible interpretation of the term might be that although the child realizes that others have visual percepts which may differ from his own, he lacks the necessary skills for predicting what these may be.

The next problem is to elucidate this: what does it mean when we say 'a child lacks the skills for predicting another's view'? From the study of Masangkay *et al.* (1974) we know that 2½- and 3-year-olds can state verbally which picture is visible to themselves and which to an experimenter sitting on the opposite side of a vertically-positioned card. In this sense, then, the young child does possess the ability to predict another's view: he can use verbal labels to represent the other's view. In the task used by Masangkay *et al.* pictures of *familiar* objects (e.g. cat, dog) were used; because these words should already be available to the child the task should be fairly simple. Perhaps, then, the reason for children's failure on the three-mountains task is due to lack of familiarity with the task material. Using familiar objects as the stimulus material, Borke (1975) showed that many three- and four-year-olds are capable of predicting another person's view. As well as a three-mountains-type model, Borke also used displays consisting of (1) a small lake with a toy boat, (2) a toy house and car, and (3) a model house, and another containing eight different groups of toy people and animals in natural settings: (1) cowboys, Indians, and trees, (2) a lake with ducks, (3) a windmill, (4) cows pulling a wagon, (5) a dog and kennel, (6) a barn with four animals and farmer, (7) a women feeding chickens, and (8) two rabbits and a pigpen with pigs. Whereas all subjects succeeded over 80% of the time with the scenes containing familiar toy objects, three-year-olds gave only 42% correct responses and 4-year-olds gave 67% correct responses in the three-mountains task.

It is debatable whether the relative difficulty of tasks can be attributed solely to the familiarity of the stimulus material. Whereas mountains might be unfamiliar to some children, presumably to Piaget and Inhelder's subjects they would be just as familiar as farm animals, etc. Rather than the familiarity of the objects being critical it is probably the fact that animals and people present more obvious orientations (i.e. *front* view or *back* view) that makes it easier to predict another's view of them compared with the more regularly-shaped mountains. Given a group of such objects, one could select a picture to represent another's view (or turn a turntable containing a duplicate scene) solely on the basis of the orientation of only *one* object, e.g. the front of the windmill facing the observer. With the three mountains, however, there is no front, back, or side of each mountain; when predicting another's view the child is forced to consider the spatial relationships *among* the mountains; e.g. from the other observer's point of view the green one may be in the middle, the brown one on the right, the grey one on the left.

Flavell (1974) has looked again at children's performance on perspectives tasks and has suggested an explanation which dispenses with the notion of egocentrism. (Table 1 shows how Flavell's reformulation of the developmental changes in perspective-taking might fit in with those suggested by Piaget and Inhelder.)

Flavell's level 1 presumably coincides with Piaget's sensorimotor period of cognitive development in which the child is assumed not to have any means of representing objects and events either by word or image. Piaget and Inhelder, of course, have not extended their investigation of perspective-taking to this very early period of development.

When children are capable of representation (perhaps at about age 18 months or

TABLE 1
Piaget and Inhelder's stages of perspective-taking compared with Flavell's levels.

PIAGET and INHELDER (1956)	FLAVELL (1974)
	Level O Practical knowledge of space; no symbolic representation of objects.
Stage I (below 4 years) The child does not understand the questions.	**Level 1** The child can represent which objects others see but not their particular view of them.
Stage IIA (4 to 5;6 years) The child is egocentric—he cannot distinguish between his own and the doll's view.	
Stage IIB (5;6 to 7 years) Unsuccessful although he does make some attempt to separate different views.	
Stage IIIA (7 to 8;6 years) Can distinguish separate views but cannot deal with all spatial relationships simultaneously.	**Level 2** The child can represent another's view of objects which are visible both to himself and to the other observer.
Stage IIIB (8;6 to 9 or 10 years) Simultaneously deals with all changes in spatial relationships occurring with a change in perspective.	
	Level 3 The child can represent another's retinal image of an object array-projective, rather than actual sizes and shapes of objects.

two years), Flavell suggests that they are at first able to represent the particular objects which are visible to themselves and others but that they are not aware of the different views each object presents to each observer. Thus, children may know that the experimenter sees a picture of a cat whereas they themselves see a picture of a dog but they will not be conscious of any particular orientation of the animals in the pictures. If both pictures are visible to both observers then the child knows only that the two views are similar in this respect; he does not know that the orientation of the pictures may differ (i.e. the dog may be right-side-up for the child but upside-down for the experimenter).

Flavell suggests that, later, children become aware of the different orientations presented by objects to both observers. Much later still, children may be able to consider the *apparent* size and shape of objects as seen from another's viewpoint; thus, Flavell extends the sequence of development beyond that reviewed by Piaget and Inhelder.

Flavell's levels help us to see what might be going on when young children fail a perspectives task. With Piaget and Inhelder's three-mountains model all three mountains are visible from all viewpoints (although the green mountain may be considerably masked by the grey one if viewed from position C). (See Figure 2). The task, then, requires level 2 ability for its successful solution: in order to represent the other's view correctly the child must be aware that the mountains will appear in a different arrangement than they appear to him. Less advanced children will not have this understanding and will know only that all three mountains are visible to both participants. The child possessing level 1 ability will not be able to decide on *one* among a set of pictures (assuming a selection method of response is used): as far as he is concerned, he sees three mountains and so does the other observer so *any* picture may be the correct one as long as it shows all three mountains.

Yet it is generally reported in the literature that young children typically choose their *own* view in error (and, of course, this had led to the notion that they are fixated on their own view). So it seems that the evidence is not in accord with Flavell's prediction. According to Piaget and Inhelder's (1956) original account, however, children *do* choose views other than their own and are still regarded as egocentric. Unfortunately, Piaget and Inhelder give no indication of the frequency of the different types of error – i.e. own view or others – and give only a couple of illustrative examples of the second type (p. 219):

REN (7; 6) is at A and the doll at B (to the right of the model). Of each picture in turn he says, '*It's right; he takes the grey one and the green one*', then (picture I) '*He can take that one as well, he gets the green one and the brown one; it's got all the three, the brown, the green and the grey*', etc., etc. In the end he expresses a preference for those pictures which include all three mountains.

TEA (8; 1) also chooses a series of pictures for each position, one after another while saying, '*He can take all three*'. Finally he is asked which picture is most correct. Running over the ones he has picked out (he has already eliminated those showing only two mountains) he once again says, '*This one will do just as well because it's got all three*'.

It is clear then that the accounts of Piaget and Inhelder and Flavell are not in opposition; both agree that the young child may choose any picture which shows all the objects in the array. Furthermore, Salatas and Flavell (1976) showed that children do not realize that only one view is possible from one viewpoint and that observers in different locations have different views. Nevertheless, there is a strong expectation on the part of the experimenter that only one picture is required. And, there may be other constraints operating which encourage the child to select his own view rather than any other.

It would be naïve to assume that children come to the experimental setting without expectations of the task. For instance, they may construe the task as a matching game and may believe that they are *supposed* to select the picture which matches their own view. Having interpreted the situation in this way they may be unreceptive to the experimenter's instructions about representing another's point of view. Only anecdotal evidence is available here, though: some eager subjects known to the author have gleefully picked out their own view before the experimenter was able to give the instructions and said, 'That's it! That's the one that matches!'

Another reason why the child may respond with his own view is that he may not even accept the 'other' as an observer possessing a view. Cox (1975, 1977a) showed that children perform much better in a perspective-taking task when a person acts as the other observer than when a doll is used. She argued that children may not regard the doll as having a view and may therefore consider themselves as being the only observers in the situation; as a consequence, they select their own view. Fehr (1979), comparing a normal observer, a blindfolded observer, and a doll, also concluded that perspective-taking ability is diminished when the other observer is a hypothetical one.

Even if the child does accept the other observer as having a view, he may still have difficulty in keeping the view in mind (or the fact that he is supposed to be considering it); he may lapse into responding with his own view since it is perhaps more immediate to him (Flavell 1974, pp. 80–81). This is similar to Hoy's suggestion (1974) that the own-view response may be the young child's reaction to information overload rather than an inability to take another's perspective. This interpretation is supported by Eliot and Dayton's (1974) finding that even adults tend to give own-view responses in more complex tasks. They suggested that 'egocentric errors are more a function of task complexity and experience with ambiguous perceptual tasks than an inability to take another's viewpoint' (p. 16).

In conclusion, Flavell's levels of perspective-taking are not incompatible with the stages proposed by Piaget and Inhelder, but Flavell has clarified the mechanism involved. As far as the young child's ability is concerned (Piaget and Inhelder's stage IIA or Flavell's level 1) the concept of egocentrism, in the sense that it has come to be used (i.e. that the child believes another has the same view as he has), is unnecessary and misleading. With regard to the question of which skills the child needs in order to solve a perspective-taking task, Flavell argues that the child first learns which objects are visible to different observers and only later learns to deal with *how* they are seen in terms of the spatial relationships among them.

Spatial relationships in the three-mountains task

Since the three-mountains task is so well-known and has been widely used in studies of perspective-taking, we shall examine it in more detail. Given that both observers can see all the mountains in the array and that a mountain does not have an obvious front or back, in order to succeed in the task a child needs to know something about the spatial relationships among objects and how these change with a change of perspective. What we need to investigate is how this knowledge of another's view develops; in other words, Flavell's level 2 ability needs to be elucidated.

Piaget and Inhelder (1956) and Laurendeau and Pinard (1970) note that, in the three-mountains task, the child is first able to represent the dominant feature of the doll's view. The following example (Piaget and Inhelder, p. 227) illustrates what is meant by 'dominant':

> FUL (6; 10) is at A (left to right: brown, grey, green) and the doll near D (grey, green, brown). Seen from A the most striking feature of the doll's position is that it is close to the grey mountain. FUL, therefore, chooses a picture with the grey mountain in the foreground but to the right, with the green to the left and the brown hidden by the green. 'Why that one? – *It will do; the grey one's in front. He's right near the grey one. He sees it first and here it's first as well*'.

Thus, the child fixes on one particular feature of the other's view, but ignores the arrangement of the other objects. In fact, the feature most salient in the other's view seems to be the object nearest to the observer. Cox (1978a and b) found this to be the case with six-year-olds who had just begun to be able to predict another's view accurately. Harris and Bassett's (1976) findings also support this first step in perspective-taking: even though six-year-olds may reconstruct their own view and attribute it to the other observer, they begin the reconstruction with the element which corresponds with that nearest the other observer.

A further step in the child's understanding of spatial relationships, according to Piaget and Inhelder, is his ability to represent correctly objects arranged one behind another from another observer's perspective. And last, he is able to represent correctly objects arranged in a left–right relationship with respect to another's viewpoint. Piaget and Inhelder's explanation for this before–behind/left–right order of acquisition is that 'there is a bigger difference between a background beyond the reach of immediate action and a foreground directly subject to it, than there is between a left and right which are equally near or distant'. Indeed, there is a considerable body of literature on the difficulty of left–right concepts (e.g. Benton, 1959; Elkind, 1961) which would lead one to expect that left–right relationships would be particularly difficult in a perspective-taking task also. But, Piaget and Inhelder did not carry out any statistical analysis of their data and no further experiment was conducted to test this order-of-acquisition hypothesis; the order of mastery of these relationships was the conclusion of a *post hoc* analysis of the children's verbal descriptions of what a doll could see rather than of a systematic investigation. Subsequently, however, a number of studies have provided evidence for these steps in perspective-taking.

Coie, Costanzo and Farnill (1973) asked subjects (aged 8 to 10 years in one experiment and aged 5; 10 to 10; 4 years in another) to select a doll's view from various positions around a group of three houses. The types of errors made were examined. The results provided evidence that 'interposition' errors are the first type of error to be eliminated. (This before–behind error is made when a child fails to recognize that some parts of an array are partially hidden when viewed from another's position.) The second type of error to be eliminated are those of 'orientation', i.e. a failure to infer that another person has a corner view, a side view or a frontal view of the objects in the array. The ability to reconstruct right–left relationships between objects as they would appear from another's perspective is very difficult and the last type of error to be eliminated.

Whereas Coie *et al.* used familiar objects – houses – which possess easily-recognizable sides (e.g. front, back), Nigl and Fishbein (1973) used arrays made up of featureless, geometrical solids. Again, it was found that left–right relationships are much more difficult than before–behind relationships.

Cox (1978a and b) also used arrays containing featureless objects and found that after the child first represents another's view by correctly locating the object nearest to the other observer, he later correctly locates the object behind the first one (in other words, he can correctly represent objects arranged in a before–behind relationship as seen by the other observer); last, he correctly represents the left–right arrangement of objects as seen by the other observer.

A problem with these studies, however, is that they included before–behind and left–right relationships in the same object array. Where both relationships are presented simultaneously, a greater number of left–right errors may not necessarily indicate that left–right relationships are more difficult than before–behind ones. It may be that children prefer to deal with the before–behind relationship first and neglect the left–right relationship, possibly because limitations in their 'central computing space' (Pascual-Leone, 1970) prevent both relationships being simultaneously combined.

What is needed, therefore, in order to test the relative difficulty of before–behind and left–right relationships is an experiment in which these object-arrangements are presented separately. In fact there are three studies which have done this. Tanaka (1968) used a bowling pin and a ball and presented them either one behind the other or one beside the other. The child was required to predict a doll's view of the objects, and it was found that the before–behind arrangement was easier than the side-by-side arrangement.

Minnigerode and Carey (1974) also found that children concentrated more on before–behind relationships and neglected left–right ones. For the before–behind arrays, they used a mountain and a house, and for the left–right arrays a mountain and a tree. The design of the experiment would have been neater if the same objects had been used for both types of spatial relationship. In addition to this perhaps rather minor criticism, the order of presentation of the two types of spatial arrangement was not randomized: the left–right arrangement was always presented first and the before–behind arrangement second. The conclusion that before–behind relationships are easier is therefore suspect; they might be easier simply because of a practice effect.

Unfortunately, no information is given in the Tanaka paper about the order of presentation. Hoy (1974), however, was careful to randomize the order of her tasks and found that before–behind relationships were easier than left–right. Thus, Piaget and Inhelder's contention that 'before–behind relationships become reversible, and consequently more responsive to changes of perspective, sooner than those of left and right' (pp. 235–236) appears to be supported.

A problem with all these studies cited above regarding the relative difficulty of spatial relationships is that even when the order of presentation has been controlled the amount of masking has not. When objects are arranged side-by-side neither one masks the other; but, when objects are presented in a before–behind relationship the front one masks the one behind it. This occlusion may be partial as in the Tanaka and Hoy studies or total as in the Minnigerode and Carey experiment. We have already seen from Flavell's work on the development of perspective-taking skills that young children may find it easier to specify *which* objects another sees rather than *how* the same objects are seen by himself and another observer. In Flavell's (1974) terms, representing a view in which one object masks another involves level 1 ability whereas level 2 ability is required to represent a view in which all the objects are visible to both the other observer and the child. The before–behind arrangements presented in the aforementioned studies should therefore be easier than the left–right arrangements because they involved partial or total masking whereas the left–right arrangements involved no masking.

In order to circumvent this difficulty one might present both arrangements so that neither involves any masking, i.e. as two-dimensional arrays flat on the table rather than as three-dimensional solid objects. A recent experiment (Cox and Willetts, in preparation) demonstrates that absence of masking in the object array results in equal performance for before–behind and left–right arrangements.

This problem of masking *versus* no masking has also confounded the findings regarding the relative difficulty of different viewpoints. In fact there is conflicting evidence in the literature: Laurendeau and Pinard (1970) and Eiser (1974) found that children made fewer errors when the other observer sat opposite them than at the sides, but Nigl and Fishbein (1973) found that more errors were made for the opposite position than for the sides.

First of all these studies can be criticized because the arrangement of the objects was not the same for each view. Obviously, if the objects present a different arrangement when viewed from the side compared with the opposite position this variable alone could be responsible for the relative difficulty of the positions. But the degree of masking was a more pertinent confounding variable: in the Laurendeau and Pinard (1970) and Eiser (1974) studies, for example, whereas the largest object masked the smallest one when the array was viewed from the opposite side, *all* objects were visible from the side positions. It is not surprising, then, that the opposite view was easier in these studies. Cox (1977b) in an experiment which controlled both the object arrangement and the degree of masking for each view found that the opposite view was more difficult to represent correctly than the side views.

In summary, recent experimental research has investigated in more detail how the child's ability to predict another's view of a group of objects develops; this has involved a study of the types of spatial relationships among objects and the relative difficulty with which they can be manipulated. Generally speaking, the findings support Piaget and Inhelder's rather sketchy observations.

General summary

The young child's difficulty in predicting another's view in a perspective-taking task is frequently cited as evidence for his basic egocentric view of the world. Recent experimental investigations of perspective-taking have shown that although the young child's abilities are limited and he only gradually develops the skills necessary to represent another's view in any detailed way, he is far from being 'egocentric' in the commonly accepted sense of the term.

References

BENTON, A. L. (1959) *Right–Left Discrimination and Finger Localization*. Hoeber-Harper.

BORKE, H. (1975) 'Piaget's mountains revisited: changes in the egocentric landscape'. *Developmental Psychology*, **11**, 240–243.

BRAINE, M. D. S. (1962) 'Piaget on reasoning: A methodological critique and alternative proposals'. In KESSEN, W. and KUHLMAN, C. (Eds.) *Thought in the Young Child. Monographs of the Society for Research in Child Development*, **27**, 41–61.

COIE, J. D., COSTANZO, P. R. and FARNILL, D. (1973) 'Specific transitions in the development of spatial perspective-taking ability'. *Developmental Psychology*, **9**, 167–177.

COX, M. V. (1975) 'The other observer in a perspectives task'. *British Journal of Educational Psychology*, **45**, 83–85.

COX, M. V. (1977a) 'Perspective ability: the other observer in the task'. *Perceptual and Motor Skills*, **44**, 76.

COX, M. V. (1977b) 'Perspective ability: the relative difficulty of the other observer's viewpoints. *Journal of Experimental Child Psychology*, **24**, 254–259'.

COX, M. V. (1978a) 'Order of the acquisition of perspective-taking skills'. *Developmental Psychology*, **14**, 421–422.

COX, M. V. (1978b) 'The development of perspective-taking ability in children'. *International Journal of Behavioral Development*, **1**, 247–254.

DONALDSON, M. (1978) *'Children's Minds'*. Glasgow: Fontana.

EISER, C. (1974) 'Recognition and inference in the coordination of perspectives'. *British Journal of Educational Psychology*, **44**, 309–312.

ELIOT, J. and DAYTON, C. M. (1976) 'Egocentric error and the construct of egocentrism'. *Journal of Genetic Psychology*, **128**, 275–289.

ELKIND, D. (1961) 'Children's conceptions of right and left: Piaget replication study IV'. *Journal of Genetic Psychology*, **99**, 269–276.

FEHR, L. A. (1979) 'Hypotheticality and the other observer in a perspective task'. *British Journal of Educational Psychology*, **49**, 93–96.

FLAVELL, J. H. (1974) 'The development of inferences about others'. In MISCHEL, T. (Ed.) *Understanding Other Persons*. Oxford: Blackwell.

FLAVELL, J. H., SHIPSTEAD, S. G. and CROFT, K. (1978) 'Young children's knowledge about visual perception: hiding objects from others'. *Child Development*, **49**, 1208–1211.

HALL, E. (1970) 'A conversation with Jean Piaget and Bärbel Inhelder'. *Psychology Today*, **3**, 25–32 and 54–56.

HARRIS, P. L. and BASSETT, E. (1976) 'Reconstruction from the mental image'. *Journal of Experimental Child Psychology*, **21**, 514–523.

HOY, E. A. (1974) 'Predicting another's visual perspective: a unitary skill?' *Development Psychology*, **10**, 462.

HUTTENLOCHER, J. and PRESSON, C. C. (1973) 'Mental rotation and the perspective problem'. *Cognitive Psychology*, **4**, 277–299.

KURDEK, L. A. and RODGON, M. M. (1975) 'Perceptual, cognitive, and affective perspective taking in kindergarten through sixth-grade children'. *Developmental Psychology*, **11**, 643–650.

LAURENDEAU, M. and PINARD, A. (1970) *The Development of the Concept of Space in the Child*. New York: International Universities Press.

LEMPERS, J. D., FLAVELL, E. R. and FLAVELL, J. H. (1977) 'The development in very young children of tacit knowledge concerning visual perception'. *Genetic Psychology Monographs*, **95**, 3–53.

MASANGKAY, Z. S., McCLUSKEY, K. A., McINTYRE, C. W., SIMS-KNIGHT, J., VAUGHN, B. E. and FLAVELL, J. H. (1974) 'The early development of inferences about the visual percepts of others'. *Child Development*, **45**, 357–366.

MINNIGERODE, F. A. and CAREY, R. N. (1974) 'Development of mechanisms underlying spatial perspectives'. *Child Development*, **45**, 496–498.

NIGL, A. J. and FISHBEIN, H. D. (1973) 'Children's ability to co-ordinate perspectives: cognitive factors (1)'. In PREISER, W. F. E. (Ed.) *Environmental Design Research. Vol. 2.* Stroudsburg, Pennsylvania: Dowden, Hutchinson and Ross.

PASCUAL-LEONE, J. (1970) 'A mathematical model for the transition rule in Piaget's developmental stages'. *Acta Psychologica*, **32**, 301–345.

PIAGET, J. and INHELDER, B. (1956) *The Child's Conception of Space.* London: Routledge and Kegan Paul.

PIAGET, J. and INHELDER, B. (1959) *The Language and Thought of the Child.* London: Routledge and Kegan Paul.

PIAGET, J. and INHELDER, B. (1971) *Mental Imagery in the Child: a Study of the Development of Imaginal Representation.* London: Routledge and Kegan Paul.

SALATAS, H. and FLAVELL, J. H. (1976) 'Perspective taking: the development of two components of knowledge'. *Child Development*, **47**, 103–109.

SHANTZ, C. U. and WATSON, J. S. (1970) 'Assessment of spatial egocentrism through expectancy violation'. *Psychonomic Science*, **18**, 93–94.

STRAUSS, S. and COHEN, J. (1974) 'A study of the relations between mental operations underlying rotation and perspective tasks'. Unpublished manuscript, Tel-Aviv University.

TANAKA, Y. (1968) 'Children's representation of spatial transformation'. *Japanese Journal of Educational Psychology*, **16**, 124 (Abstract in English.).

5

The underlying order in children's drawings

NORMAN FREEMAN

Symptoms of egocentrism

Some drawings are set out in Figure 1. They form a queer collection. They are certainly childish, and if egocentrism is a necessary aspect of children's life, surely these ought to provide symptoms. Some of the drawings appear to be incomplete, some to be peculiarly organized, and some seem both incomplete and queerly organized. These characteristics give what Piaget (1928), in his opening pages, called a 'discontinuous and chaotic character' to the 'idiom' or representation of young children. Piaget uses the cover term 'synthetic incapacity' to mean that parts are juxtaposed instead of being related one to another. He states that this is the 'mark of the whole of childish thought' in young children. So according to Piaget, such drawings give immediate access to the jumbled nature of children's thought-processes. This is an important claim. Can the characteristics of representational thought be printed out on a page? It would be nice if they could, but I shall argue that they cannot. So all we have to do in the first part of this chapter is to ask whether the chaotic surface appearance of drawings conceals an underlying orderliness which is of more fundamental interest; and to see whether the concept of egocentrism can help us to understand either the underlying processes, the appearance of the finished products or the relationship between the processes and the products. To do the job properly would take many pages, but fortunately I have laboured away at these recently (Freeman, 1980), and so here we can just go straight to the essentials and leave all the convolutions on one side. Most of the points made in this chapter can be tracked down in my book. We start with modes of thought and egocentrism according to Piaget.

If the tendency to juxtapose items instead of organizing them into disciplined relationships really be a mode of operation, what holds it back from ruining the children's development? Do they never try to relate things together? The answer is that of course they do, but, again according to Piaget (1928, p. 4) they tend to fall over into a tendency to 'connect everything with everything else'. This he calls 'syncretism', and describes it as an 'excess of relating while juxtaposition exhibits a deficiency in the same function'. So here are two marks of childish representation,

Fig. 1 Sample of young children's drawings

set out in the opening pages of Piaget's important book, with the suggestion that one examines drawings to see them clearly in operation.

Piaget picks up the story again on page 58 of his book. The characteristics of thought and of drawing are perfectly comparable; and he goes on to say that juxtaposition and syncretism are not only complementary but alternate over indefinite periods in the individual. Figure 2 shows a set of drawings from Sarah. Do the two modes seem to alternate at all? I'm not convinced that they do. But anyway, we now come to the heart of the matter: 'Egocentric thought is necessarily syncretic' says Piaget on page 228. Egocentrism is supposed to produce syncretism and its converse, juxtaposition. How does it do so? By substituting subjectivity for a representation of objective relations. Of course this appears in drawings, for the child's picture of the world is shown in his drawings not as objects really are 'but as he would have imagined them' (Piaget, 1928, p. 249). This used to be called 'intellectual realism' as opposed to 'visual realism' (Freeman, 1972, for a critique of these concepts). So the child is trying to be realistic, but his subjectivity inexorably obtrudes. This, with reasonable fidelity, is the view reiterated by Piaget and Inhelder as late as 1969 in their comments on drawing.

Now to sum up. According to Piaget, the child is extremely subjective in representing objective reality, up to the age of seven or eight years; and this will be manifest as a tendency to relate too many things together so as to construct an overinclusive whole, as well as a tendency to lapse into failures to respect relationships and to produce a juxtaposed jumble of parts. This may or may not tell us why the drawings look peculiar. It will certainly not tell us how they are produced. In fact, oddly enough, in all the pages produced by Piaget over a number of years, there is only a very small number which specify how the processes of production of a drawing may be presumed to operate. Does this not tell us that something is liable to be wrong with the story? An account which passes global judgements on the finished products without telling us how they got that way is surely in danger of missing the point entirely.

What is the crucial point? Again, let us return to Piaget (1928) for a glimpse of it. On page 128 he suggests how a child might go about drawing a bicycle. The child summons up representations of the parts which both exist and have a name in his repertoire, such as wheels or pedals, and 'is content' to draw them side by side, not troubling himself about their method of contact. How can Piaget possibly know whether the child 'is content' to ignore the spatial relations? Had he himself never tried to draw a bicycle? A good recipe for discontented syncretism or juxtaposition in adults, anyway, is to ask them to draw simple machines. The results are often the products of heroic failed efforts. Clearly, an adequate account of drawing has to focus on the *relationship* between the processes of production and the form of the product. When Piaget was writing, there was very little experimental evidence on how people go about organizing information in a form which would enable them to give a coherent output. Nowadays we know a great deal about the obstacles which a person meets when trying to programme action. Often a tiny hitch in the programming can lead to a really messy output. How can one go about distinguishing the dramatic effects of tiny hitches in ordered thought from the dramatic effects of disorderly thought? Here follow some recipes for so doing in the area of children's drawing. The results lead one to shift the concept of egocentrism away from the central position as a 'mark of childish thought'. First we deal with evidence which shifts the concept, then we shall have to work out quite what has become of it.

Organizing a complex drawing

The drawings set out in the previous two Figures could, if one wanted to, be put on a grid of juxtaposition and syncretism. Some of them seem to have too few relationships depicted, others to have things wrongly, indeed extravagantly, related. But I am now going to show that appearances can be very deceptive. The argument goes as follows.

First, what do we compare the drawings with? It would be absurd to compare them with real people. Of course one cannot capture the complexity of a real person in three dimensions on a tiny piece of paper. One constructs a transformation of the structure of the person. In doing this, certain things have to be omitted, and others

83

Fig. 2 A sequence of pictures from Sarah during four days at the age of four years nine months. What principle could economically encompass such diversity in methods of construction? (**a**) Square birds with worms in their beaks flying to the nest with two baby birds on top of a smiling tree. The house contains a mantelpiece with ornaments. (**b**) Hedgehog (**c**) Kite-flying (**d**) Football (**e**) Ping-pong (**f**) Batman and Robin (**g**) Train, car and horse-rider

(a)

(b)

(c)

(d)

(e)

(f)

(g)

have to be transformed according to quite disciplined rules. Notice the early use of a single line to represent a limb. This is a transformation rule of a very high order of abstraction indeed: an object is reduced to a collapsed pair of contours. Immediately, the selection of this graphic convention has its consequences. For instance, it is not possible to represent the relationship between shoulder and arm, or wrist and hand. These points are surely obvious. But what is of interest is the less obvious point that the choice of graphic conventions always inevitably has organizational consequences. If Piaget were right in assuming that the child draws by summoning up discrete items from memory and choosing a graphic form for each separate item, then certain modes of organization and disorganization would inevitably follow whatever the child's level of synthetic ability. Without some theory of graphic vocabulary one cannot have an index of the degrees of freedom to organize that are at the child's disposal. There are a few glimmerings of what such a theory might look like to be found in the writings of Arnheim (1956), Kellogg (1970), Goodnow (1977), and Freeman (1980). But no more than glimmerings, unfortunately.

Second, suppose Piaget to be right in his notion that the child begins drawing by summoning up discrete named items from an internal store. This in itself has organizational consequences. Imagine what would happen if you began drawing a bicycle by following Piaget's list, which begins with wheels. If you put them too close together, you would have great difficulty in organizing the rest no matter how good your intentions. Putting them too far apart would be bad too. In brief, you would only do well if you could do a great deal of *advance planning* using a complex internal store to good effect, and relating the order of production over time to the disposition of the items in space on the page. It is quite conceivable that young children have good internal representations but lack the control skills necessary to sustain advance planning throughout the whole course of the drawing. In such a case, what could they do? They would be forced to use local landmark cues on the page to construct the drawing, and would have periodically to make wild corrections to get the local configurations into shape to form a whole. From my experience watching children drawing, I think that this is often what they do; and to me, this is a better way of thinking about their problems than to imagine that they veer between juxtaposition and syncretism. It is essential to distinguish between the children's awareness of specific relationships and their ability to write themselves a production programme which will hold the method of depicting them for long enough to guide the whole course of the drawing.

Advance planning is necessary for all drawings without exception. It is necessary for each aspect of any drawing too. Thus, if you are drawing a human figure by starting with the head, if that be drawn too close to one side of the page (usually the left hand side) that will restrict one side of the rest of the drawing; and if the head be drawn too expansively on the blank page, that will lead to complications in getting the size-relations of the rest in harmony with it. We take these points for granted, but they have to be learned by young children over an extensive number of trials, errors and spontaneous experiments. Who can teach them what degree of advance planning is necessary at each stage? Drawing is a relatively solitary activity, and most of the rules have painfully to be worked out by the children themselves. It is not as though objective reality provides a set of checks and balances in the way that it does when playing with bricks say. You can see a tower of bricks fall over if you place one wrongly; but the consequences of drawing a line in the wrong place may not be manifest at the time, and only have consequences much later in the drawing sequence. Piaget has surely underestimated how difficult it is for children to teach themselves to draw.

Now we are in a position to look for the hidden orderliness which may lie concealed beneath the surface symptoms of egocentrism. The task is to look for the methods of planning children use, so that we can separate the reliable relationships which they portray from the unreliable juxtapositions and syncretisms. In the case of human figure drawing, this is a simple task, and the argument runs as follows.

First, consider the vast amount of survey data which people have collected on the frequency of body parts. The earliest one which is at all in harmony with subsequent ones is, I think, that of Partridge (1902). In her sample the trunk was included in 50% of the four-year-olds' drawings, 82% of the five-year-olds' and 92% of the six-year-olds'. The figures for the legs were 39%, 83%, 92% respectively; for the arms, 45%, 67%, 71% respectively and for the neck, 8%, 22%, 20% respectively. Thus the development of the figure is initially a head, then a head with limbs (called a 'tadpole form'), a head with a trunk and limbs, and finally a head, limbs, trunk and neck. Of course, there is tremendous variation between children, and even in the same child's productions from hour to hour. But these general trends hold good for a large number of surveys, except that all the others find the legs to be more reliably drawn than arms at all ages between three and six years. In general then, it is useful to note that the trunk and arms are less reliably represented than other items of the groundplan of the human figure.

Why might this be? One possibility is that they owe their unreliability to their spatial position. The middle of any series tends to be less well represented than the ends. This is one of the most familiar findings in the study of human performance, and it comes up across an immense number of tasks. In general, if one wishes to assess the accuracy of relational representation, look to the ends of any series for evidence.

This actually fits in beautifully with Piaget's suggestion about how a topic might be drawn. If, as he argues, the child samples from a list of features, one expects things to go wrong around the middle of the list. A tendency to end-anchor on the head and legs would be a rational strategy. It enables the child to launch the drawing; but its very success inevitably leads to organizational problems with the middle of the drawing. It is possible to chart the course of children's struggles with the ordering problems by observing the temporal order in which they draw the items. Early drawings tend to be constructed in the order head–legs, or head–legs–arms; then this gives way to head–trunk–legs, or head–trunk–legs–arms; and finally the adult order of head–trunk–arms–legs only reliably appears around the age of five or six years. Again, one has to say that a problem of programming action intervenes between the mental image and the graphic image: whatever the children know about the graphic relationships to be constructed, they will be liable to run into difficulties until they can do the advance planning necessary to make the temporal order of production map on to the spatial order on the page.

Now we have the elements of a theory of drawing in the above remarks. Children have a problem when they select which items to depict, they will run into problems with intermediate items, they have a temporal-spatial mapping problem to handle, and they must conduct advance planning. Can these help us study the peculiar organization of the human figure? The answer is that they can, since all we have to do to launch an experimental programme is to provide preschool children with different types of incomplete figure designed so as to provide planning cues which they themselves apparently cannot provide when struggling with a blank page. For example, the trunk has been identified as a point of difficulty: what now will happen if we provide a predrawn head and trunk and ask the children to complete the figure? As expected, they put legs reliably at the bottom of the figure, even if they themselves have had the habit of spontaneously adding legs to the head in their own drawings. So they have a grasp of the rule that legs define the bottom of the drawing. But the arms give rise to a totally different pattern of behaviour: they tend to be positioned on whichever is the larger, the head or the trunk. In fact, it is easy to get individual tadpole-drawers to vacillate, and to alternate between drawing arms on the head or on the trunk, by giving successive drawings with the head alternating as the larger or smaller of the two. It is not the absolute size of the head or trunk which controls the positioning tendency, but the ratio of the two. I have called this 'the body proportion effect'. It turns out to be a most robust effect indeed, and one which is proof against many types of potential competing factors. For example, it is unaffected by asking the children to draw a navel on the trunk first: they draw it accurately then still position the arms on the larger of the two gross body segments (Freeman and Hargreaves, 1977). In some sense, they know what they are doing, queer though the doing be.

So here we have a local cue to action which is different from that used by adults. It is a reliably-used cue which the children use as a place-holder for the difficult intermediate item of the groundplan of the drawing. It is arguable that a trace of it is still discernible at eight years of age, if one's observation techniques are fine enough (the evidence can be found under the entry *Body proportion effect: fine positioning*, in my book). Whatever the final explanation of the effect, all we are concerned with here is its status: it is an orderly rule which cannot be subsumed under either juxtaposition or syncretism, and which is associated with a phase of active production of many apparently chaotic forms in the children's idiom of the time.

Now we can evaluate the position we have reached on the edge of this uncharted area. Children's drawings of the human figure do look chaotic and egocentric to many adults. But there is a perfectly good reason for the chaos. Drawing is difficult and involves advance planning. Surely some part of the chaos is attributable to the difficulties of mastering the medium and acting in a planned manner. In short, when we succeed in analysing the task-demands of drawing a given topic, some part of the chaos will be explicable as the product of alternative coping strategies in a difficult situation. Next we can add that another part of the chaos and variation might be attributable to local cues which are perfectly orderly, like the body proportion effect. These will have to be dug for through active experimentation. These two lines of consideration make sense of some of the apparent disorder. Accordingly it is an open question whether one will want to use the term egocentrism in describing the disorder which will not yield to task-demand and local-cue analyses. I do not see why one should want to have a vested interest in the eventual answer.

To end this section, here is another example of orderliness, which brings in the point made much earlier that the choice of graphic vocabulary itself has organizational consequences. When experimenting upon the body proportion effect, we used a wide variety of figures. Only one type suddenly gave rise to a new effect. This was a set of stick figures. Here the head is a circle and the trunk a single straight line: two extremely different graphic conventions for representing solid objects. What happened when the children were asked to attach arms, was that they polarized. Some of them always repeatedly went for the head and some went for the trunk, regardless of the head-trunk ratio, with only a tiny minority still showing the body proportion effect. We do not yet know what determines the polarization, why some individuals should go for the head whilst others go for the trunk, but here is a consistent rule operated by the same children who show the body proportion effect when both head and trunk are circles, items of the same graphic vocabulary. It would be surprising if this tiny beginning could not yield a set of orderly rules operated by young children under different conditions. The lesson is now clear for the future: any instances of too little or too much relating are open to experimentation to find whether hidden rules are at work. There is, of course, an excellent precedent in modern work in psycholinguistics. There is as much raw material of study in non-linguistic representation.

Use of the external frame of reference of a picture

The previous section dealt with problems of organizing performance, and with a new method of probing alternative rules which might be at work. In itself I do not think that such work can ever settle the question of the existence of egocentrism, but only set limits to the extent to which one feels inclined to deploy the concept. The main lesson to be drawn from the previous work is that drawing is such a difficult field of action that children cannot give a simple print-out of their internal representations, be their intentions never so good. In this section we shall study what has been taken to be a specific symptom of egocentric organization, and conclude that the same lessons have to apply as in the previous section.

Again the work stems from Piaget. In one of his most important empirical reports, written with Inhelder in 1948 (translated into English in 1956), he puts forward a key instance of egocentric organization. He argued that children base their view of spatial relationships upon their own position, and it will take a great intellectual effort for them to break away from this to relying upon the whole of the external frame of reference instead. This issue has been discussed in earlier chapters in this book, by Gavin Bremner and Maureen Cox. It seems that young children do not have to be confined to using themselves as a reference point under several conditions. But many of the demonstrations merely stop there. They do not tell us how sensitively the children can use the external frame of reference when they have broken away. In short, it is one thing to show that a self-referent coding does not operate as great a tyranny as Piaget supposed, but another to show what degree of contextual sensitivity the liberated children can deploy. Here again, a drawing task ought to fit the bill, and at first sight the results are amazingly egocentric.

Piaget asked young children to draw the water level in a tilted bottle. This ought to be horizontal, paralleling the ground. But the children, according to Piaget, showed an immense tendency to draw the water level tilted. Did they not appreciate the external horizontal reference axis? Again, when invited to draw trees on a predrawn mountainside, these too would be drawn tilted. Did they not therefore appreciate the external vertical reference axis? Piaget's case rests on these two observations. He states that there comes a time when *both* the horizontal and vertical reference cues are used together, and that this co-incides with the ability to be non-egocentric in a three-mountain task. So the horizontal-vertical drawing tasks lie at the heart of the egocentrism debate.

Figure 3 shows a drawing of a house with a tilted chimney. The failure to respect the external vertical axis appears also in spontaneous drawings. But it is obvious that the chimney is not tilted at random. It forms a right-angle with the roof. So we are alerted to the possibility that a perpendicular relationship is being substituted for the parallel relationship that ought to obtain with the external reference line, and this raises a most interesting possibility. Whenever a highly stereotyped relationship

Fig. 3   The Chimney on Sarah's house is perpendicular to the roof

appears in place of the other, it is possible that this is an index of a masking bias, one that hides a deeper responsiveness to the external reference, and one which the children do not know sufficiently how to inhibit. In such a case, one must be careful not to conflate an awareness of the role of the external frame of reference with its actual use, for the test would not be an optimal one for tapping awareness of the external reference. It is easy to show that this is precisely what has happened with Piaget's test. Through no fault of his own, he had run straight into the worst possible situation for assessing awareness of wide referential coordinations. The demonstration runs as follows.

Ibbotson and Bryant (1976) gave young children a copying task. A target line was shown at an acute angle to a baseline, and the children were asked to draw the target on to a baseline of their own. The results were clear. The children could only draw an acute angle accurately when the baseline was a vertical one. A tilted baseline tended to give rise to a perpendicularization of the target line upon it. We have replicated this, and although one does not always obtain a full-blown right-angle error, it is with monotonous regularity that one sees an attraction towards the perpendicular whenever a tilted baseline is involved. This means that the majority of children up to the age of six or so, cannot draw an acute angle when they want to, even though the target line may happen to be horizontally or vertically off the tilted baseline. How then can one expect them to draw vertical trees or horizontal water levels off tilted baselines in the Piagetian task? Surely a precondition for assessing the results of the Piagetian task is some prior evidence that the children have a control of the design skills necessary to execute the drawing in accordance with their intentions. Without that, the gap between intention and performance could be wide. The existence of the perpendicular error shows that any test of responsiveness to external reference axes must remove the masking bias early on in the test.

This has been a very brief note of the bias. In my book I report the results of a number of people's attempts to mitigate its effects by various means, such as giving an additional parallelism cue or reducing the size of the baseline. All fail. The bias is a most robust one indeed whenever a tilted baseline is involved. I do not think that there is much chance of salvaging Piaget's test.

So we need a new test of responsiveness to the external frame of reference when constructing angles in drawings. Under what conditions can it be presumed that children have a control over their orientation judgements? One useful suggestion was made by Goodnow and Friedman (1972) when observing human figure drawing. They suggest that tilted drawings often result from an initial slip in drawing the eyes: if the axis of these be accidentally tilted out of the horizontal, young children will often draw the rest of the figure tilted in order to correspond with the eyes. Another way of putting it is, of course, that here we have a case of the perpendicular bias, operating between the eyes-axis and the trunk–legs axis. The only question is whether this particular occurrence of the bias is also strong enough to mask responsiveness to the vertical reference axis entirely. It turns out, for some reason, that it is not. We have given human figure drawing-completion games to a large number of young children. We drew eyes at various angles on the page, and also gave tilted pages as contexts. The results were very beautiful. Even three-year-olds would clearly monitor both the eyes-axis tilt and the page-tilt and draw the trunk and legs in a compromise orientation. This is very sophisticated behaviour indeed.

The conclusion is clearly that drawing tasks have to be handled with caution. As yet, we know very little about the ingredients for a sensitive test of contextual responsiveness, as I term it. The perpendicular bias is something which can blanket contextual responsiveness; and Piaget's task may be regarded as merely giving evidence on the bias. But, it may be argued, the very existence of the bias is a sort of egocentrism. That is possible. But the assertion would change the argument from that of Piaget. That does not mean that the argument would be wrong, of course, but it would mean that a new mode of investigation would be necessary.

For a start, the extent of the perpendicular bias would have to be mapped over a wide range of tasks. Goodnow (1978) has published a helpful note on perpendicular relations. And Byrne (1979) shows how readily adults too can lose orientation information in drawings and just turn out perpendicular relationships. So either adults too are rather egocentric, or we have here a special case of relative loss of information which does not really address the question of the subject's awareness of the role of the external frame of reference. I think that this latter possibility is the more likely one. Young children may indeed have a poor grasp of the external frame of reference, but a test which elicits the perpendicular bias is unlikely to give us a *measure* of that.

In conclusion, tests which use drawing as a type of performance will have to be designed with a much better understanding of how difficult it is to draw than was available in Piaget's time. This is not too surprising a conclusion. It is clear that Piaget's task underestimates children, but we do not yet know how badly it does so. The issue of egocentrism as dealt with in this section stands or falls by some such assessment being made. For once I do not feel that it is evading the issue to call for further work on drawing before jumping to put drawing to use as a putative symptom of deeper thought processes. At least the outline of the work to be done is fairly clear. One compiles a list of drawing tasks, in which an acute angle has to be correctly constructed, along a sort of continuum: from those which reveal acute contextual sensitivity (e.g. Naeli and Harris, 1976), through those such as the tilted human task mentioned which demonstrate both internal and contextual orientation coordination in the presence of perpendicular relations, to those in which the perpendicular bias clearly masks contextual responsiveness as in the Piaget type of task. This should give us a set of working tools.

As a final note, many readers might be reminded of the rod-and-frame test by my remarks about the tilted human figure drawing task. There is a similarity. But I must make two points. The first is that the rod-and-frame test itself is coming in for new scrutiny (see for example, Sigman, Goodenough and Flannagan, 1979). Second, this test involves real gravitational forces instead of their possible graphic correlates. That really changes the rules of explanation involved, as I have tried to explain in my book.

Self-reference with a non-existent reference line

A great deal of the work on egocentrism has been sparked off by the three-mountains task (see Chapter 4). Children often seem unable to imagine hidden views, or so it was claimed. Now we consider a graphic analogue. In drawing a three-dimensional scene onto a flat piece of paper, do children seem to violate the scene-structure in favour of depiction governed by their own viewpoint? Figure 4 seems to be one such. It is called 'a transparency representation', or better, 'interposition'. I prefer to stress that interposition results from the failure to operate the device of hidden line elimination in the production of such drawings. Certain lines should not be drawn, yet the child fails to eliminate them, as though he were drawing everything from his own viewpoint. The question is whether this is an egocentric mode of production: a result of using a self-referent line of sight which cannot directly be drawn on a flat piece of paper.

The study of the failure to operate hidden line elimination can be divided into two topics. One deals with drawings like that in Figure 4: one object which is

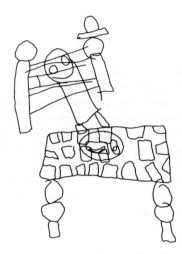

Fig. 4 The person at the table is not meant to be transparent. Therefore it is entirely wrong to call such drawings 'transparencies', just because two items have been superimposed since it is impossible for the child to draw both chair and table at once, it would require immense control to be able to operate hidden line elimination in the chairs. (Reprinted from Figure 7.3 of N. H. Freeman (1980) *Strategies of Representation in Young Children*, by permission of Academic Press).

behind another appears in its entirety despite being partially occluded in the visual scene. This is a problem in drawing a file of objects. The other topic is where a totally non-visible part of an object is shown, which could *never* be seen in a real scene no matter where your viewpoint happens to be. The interior of the human body is an example which often surprises adult viewers when they see it in a child's drawing. Legs seen through trousers is another example. These may be called 'interior drawings'. Both file-interposition and interior-interposition can be described in terms of a failure to operate hidden line elimination. Does this mean that they are psychologically equivalent? I shall now argue that they are not. File-interposition is more sensitive to actual scene-structure than is interior-interposition. This has implications for the concept of egocentrism which will be spelled out after a little consideration of the evidence.

The first step is to give a file-drawing task to young children. It does not matter whether they are asked to draw from imagination or to draw two objects set in a file away from them on a tabletop, the results are very comparable. The major age-related competitor to the operation of hidden line elimination is segregation, the tendency to keep the two objects discrete on the page (Freeman, Eiser and Sayers, 1976; Cox, 1978). So straightaway we can tentatively put forward two ideas. The first is that the so-called transparency mode of representation does not often come up if the task is a simple one: it is not a general-purpose idiom of drawing. Perhaps it only appears in special cases? The other idea is that a tendency towards segregation is a major one in young children. Now this certainly would fit a Piagetian juxtaposition scheme. This is encouraging, but a firm reminder is in order that its converse syncretism (if transparency be that) does not appear as would be essential for a full synthetic incapacity story.

The next step in the collection of evidence is to set up a situation in which the tendency towards segregation is impeded in its operation. This is easy. All one has to do is to stick the two objects together in a meaningful way. An obvious method adopted by Freeman and Janikoun (1972) was to ask children to draw a cup which had been turned so that the handle was not visible to the child. An interior-drawing mode could put the handle within the cup, a visually-faithfully mode would omit it, and the only equivalent of a segregation mode would include the handle on the side of the cup. A large number of children below the age of seven years opt for the last error. From the present point of view this has several important consequences. First, if the error of commission be an egocentric one, it is not the consequence of preserving the subjective line-of-sight on the paper, for then the interior mode would have been used. So it must be a more general egocentric error, if the concept is to be applied at all. This point will be returned to in the last section of this chapter. The second thing that follows from the demonstration is that now one can see how sensitive to alterations in the scene is the error. It turns out that if one keeps the scene-structure constant but changes its visual appearance by substituting a clear glass tankard (with a handle) for the cup, this induces more not less occurrences of the error. So here is a clear invitation to a 'transparency' drawing which the children apparently turn down in favour of a sort of segregation, if that is what the inclusion of the handle in side-view really be. This is odd because a transparency drawing would, of course, actually be visually faithful. How odd it is that previous authors have commented upon the essential childishness of transparency drawings, and yet when we begin a disciplined hunt for these, the children certainly do not embrace the opportunity to do them. Their refusal is brought out most beautifully in a paper by Light and McIntosh (1979). They asked children to draw a glass with a separate object placed behind it, and with the object inside the glass. Half the children segregated the object and the glass in the 'behind' condition, but all produced a unified drawing of the object enclosed in the glass for the 'inside' condition. So the conclusion is that segregation may well be a primitive kind of drawing device in a juxtaposition mode, but it is certainly sensitive to scene structure even when the visual appearance of the scene could encourage interior drawing. As such, segregation is an orderly tendency, whose rules of application will have to be worked out.

This now enables us to approach the question of the use of drawings as indices of communicative egocentrism. Vanessa Moore, at University College London, in her unpublished work towards a Ph.D., has been using a cup-drawing task. She shows children four cups standing in a row, and drops a sweet into one of them. It happens to have the handle turned away, as in the basic Freeman and Janikoun study. Her evidence seems to show that young children are only moderately good at drawing the target cup without its handle so as to disambiguate it from the distractors. But they seem to be even worse if they are told that the drawing will be given to the next child so that he can go straight for the sweet. A little pressure put upon the children seems to increase the stereotypy of drawing and reduce its effective information content. This happened with the first glass tankard study mentioned above. Clearly it is going to be tricky to use drawings in communicative egocentrism studies. It can be done, for Korzenik (1975) has published a neat study which shows similar things to those of the Robinsons reported in a later chapter in this book.

The conclusion, yet again, is that the concept of egocentrism helps one begin research on drawing, but that the study of drawings does not automatically provide easy access to the egocentric nature of childish thought nor do its results impel one to use the concept of egocentrism. A new area with its own rules of evidence seems to be growing in this decade. Drawing has its own logic as a system of representation: it cannot be reduced to a bundle of manual skills, nor its peculiarities ignored if one wishes to use drawings as evidence for something other than the difficulty of drawing at all.

Systems of drawing

By now it seems that one cannot readily take the characteristics of children's drawings as self-evident symptoms of gross egocentrism. There is more orderliness than at first appears lying beneath the surface of synthetic incapability, and head-on assaults on egocentric modes of failing to respect the external frame of reference, or of self-reference with a line-of-sight, have run into difficulties. At the same time, in the last section, it started to appear as though there might be some role for the concept of juxtaposition. True, it would have to be used with a scene-sensitivity tag, but it might still be utilizable. In this section we shall consider it again.

Figure 5 shows a fairly common type of drawing. This too is raw material for Piaget's diagnosis of a childish egocentric mode. The projective relations of the figures are not coordinated. That is undeniable. But yet again, is there a hidden orderliness to the drawing? Surely there is. Each of the figures is produced according to a single drawing system, namely, a use of that projection of each element which displays its characteristics most clearly. This may be called 'the canonical projection system'. Its virtue is that everything is clear. Its weakness is that certain types of relationship can be displayed, but not others. Accordingly, it now becomes possible to pose the following question: To what extent are some apparent instances of juxtaposition the product of a mode of thought which deploys

Fig. 5 Sarah, aged four years 11 months, drew this picture of a car driving to a seesaw with the people in front view and the objects in side view. What unifies the scene is that they are all in canonical projection.

a too-restricted set of relationships and to what extent are they dictated by the choice of a drawing system with consistent rules?

Here we can take a leaf out of the art historian's book. Choose any exposition of Indian or Persian art, not from any desire to draw (illegitimate) comparisons with the mentality underlying children's art, but for the purpose of asking whether the concept of a drawing system is valuable. You will quickly see how wonderfully the artists explore the possibilities of representational combinations, setting out some relationships with extreme clarity and sacrificing others. The latter are not ludicrous errors. They are the price that has to be paid for using oblique projection methods. This gives us a clue how to set to work on the overall organization of children's drawings. What has to be done is to look at what kinds of drawing system young children use, and then to see what resistance the children put up to altering the system in the face of a scene for which it will not work. The first part of the task has been started. Willats (1977) has mapped age-related changes in using drawing systems up to the level of linear perspective. The heart of that most sophisticated system is a fixed spectator viewpoint and rigorous scaling of size-distance relations. The earlier systems are not just incoherent approximations to it, but excellent systems in their own right. In my book I have tried to show how there might be a trade-off between scene-aspects that can be represented as systems develop, in particular between depth-scaling and canonical representation. One system merits particular mention here. In the vertical-perpendicular system, depth is represented almost entirely by the use of right-angles. Figure 6 shows an example. Is it possible that here is an instance of a perpendicular bias being welded into a system of its own? We shall only know when we devise a task which is designed to be soluble without more complex drawing decisions being taken, yet encourages the use of acute angles.

In conclusion, there is a new systematic approach which treats certain juxtapositions as the *consequence* of a choice of an ordered set of rules rather than

Fig. 6 A picture of Sarah's fifth birthday party. The table is drawn in a vertical-perpendicular system.

as a symptom of an inability to be rule-guided. We still do not know how conscious a strategy it is in young children to select one drawing system rather than another. Presumably one will need to do research rather like that described in the previous section which will enable one to give a scene-sensitivity tag to the implementation of one system or another. Here is a fine task for the future.

Back to Piaget ?

Up to now the concept of egocentrism has been more useful in initiating research than in providing a tool for dealing with the evidence. It might well be rather unjust to Piaget to stop there, for he has tried to take an alternative tack in his arguments in order to be more specific about mechanisms of childish thought.

He puts forward the idea (Piaget, 1951) of the mental image as a causal agent in the organization of drawing; and the mental image is based upon imitation. The child has to learn how to imitate, and then how to imitate from memory. This happens before the second year, and by then imitation 'begins to reach the level of representation' (p. 62). The child thus comes to the drawing stage already equipped with internal schemata which are relatively independent of the immediate presence of models. Models can trigger these internal representations. Perhaps this can help us understand how the glass tankard demonstration worked: the sight of a handle, even in an unfamiliar position, triggered a representation of a handle in its canonical (clearest and most customary) projection, and this was drawn in its accustomed place on the side of the glass. The use of such stereotypy is in itself egocentric in being unresponsive to the scene. But we saw that there was some degree of scene-sensitivity associated with stereotyped segregation, so the children are not absolutely egocentric. Still, some degree of egocentrism may surely be admitted.

Piaget (1951 p. 72 ff.) says that imitation operates in rather a stereotyped and egocentric manner up to the age of seven or so. This is the age at which the precursors of non-egocentrism appear, according to other writings of Piaget. Around that time, drawings give evidence on how images are embedded in the understanding. The reader who is interested in this line of argument could easily consult Piaget's books on imagery and perception (Piaget, 1961, is the most important). But when I consulted them, I simply came to one conclusion: nothing new is added about drawings, except that stereotypy is itself taken to index egocentrism. Surely this merely brings us back to the type of problem mentioned under the perpendicular bias section. Any example of apparent stereotypy could in principle be a bias which masks other alternatives in the child's repertoire. Only tireless research upon the conditions under which children can draw differently from what they usually do draw will lead us to a correct assessment of the status of drawing as a representational activity.

References

ARNHEIM, R. (1956) *Art and Visual Perception*. London: Faber and Faber.

BYRNE, R. W. (1979) Memory for urban geography. *Quarterly Journal of Experimental Psychology*, **31**, 147–154.

COX, M. V. (1978) 'Spatial depth relationships in young children's drawings'. *Journal of Experimental Child Psychology*, **26**, 551–554.

FREEMAN, N. H. (1972) 'Process and product in children's drawing'. *Perception*, **1**, 123–140.

FREEMAN, N. H. (1980) *Strategies of Representation in Young Children: Analysis of Spatial Skills and Drawing Processes*. London: Academic Press.

FREEMAN, H. H., EISER, C. and SAYERS, J. (1976) 'Children's strategies in drawing three-dimensional relationships on a two-dimensional surface'. *Journal of Experimental Child Psychology*, **23**, 305–314.

FREEMAN, N. H. and HARGREAVES, S. (1977) 'Directed movements and the body-proportion effect in preschool children's human figure drawings'. *Quarterly Journal of Experimental Psychology*, **29**, 227–235.

FREEMAN, N. H. and JANIKOUN, R. (1972) 'Intellectual realism in children's drawings of a familiar object with distinct features'. *Child Development*, **43**, 1116–1121.

GOODNOW, J. J. (1977) *Children's Drawings*. London: Fontana.

GOODNOW, J. J. (1978) 'Visible thinking: cognitive aspects of change in drawings'. *Child Development*, **49**, 637–641.

GOODNOW, J. J. and FRIEDMAN, S. (1972) 'Orientation in children's human figure drawings'. *Developmental Psychology*, 7, 10–16.

IBBOTSON, A. and BRYANT, P. E. (1976) 'The perpendicular error and the vertical effect'. *Perception*, 5, 319–326.

KELLOGG, R. (1970) *Analysing Children's Art*. Palo Alto: National Press.

KORZENIK, D. (1975) 'Changes in representation between the ages of five and seven'. *Psychiatry and Art*, 4, 95–104.

LIGHT, P. H. and MCINTOSH, E. (1979) 'Depth relationships in young children's drawings'. Internal paper, Department of Psychology, University of Southampton.

NAELI, H. and HARRIS, P. L. (1976) 'Orientation of the diamond and the square'. *Perception*, 5, 73–78.

PARTRIDGE, L. (1902) 'Children's drawings'. In BARNES, E. (Ed.) *Studies in Education*. **Vol. 2**. Philadelphia: Stanford University Press.

PIAGET, J. (1928) *Judgement and Reasoning in the Child*. Routledge and Kegan Paul.

PIAGET, J. (1951) *Play, Dreams and Imitation in Childhood*. London: Routledge and Kegan Paul.

PIAGET, J. (1961) *The Mechanisms of Perception*. London: Routledge and Kegan Paul. (English translation published 1969.)

PIAGET, J. and INHELDER, B. (1948) *The Child's Conception of Space*. London: Routledge and Kegan Paul. (English translation published 1956.)

PIAGET, J. and INHELDER, B. (1969) *The Psychology of the Child*. London: Routledge and Kegan Paul.

SIGMAN, E., GOODENOUGH, D. R. and FLANNAGAN, M. (1979) 'Instructions, illusory self-tilt and the rod-and-frame test'. *Quarterly Journal of Experimental Psychology*, 31, 155–165.

WILLATS, J. (1977) 'How children learn to represent three-dimensional space in drawings'. In BUTTERWORTH, G. E. (Ed.) *The Child's Representation of the World*. London: Plenum Press.

6

Egocentrism in verbal referential communication

E. J. ROBINSON AND W. P. ROBINSON

Introduction

Piaget draws a distinction between older children who are aware of problems involved in the achievement of successful communication, and younger children who are not aware: '... we believe that the age at which the child begins to communicate his thoughts ... is probably somewhere between seven and eight. This does not mean that from the age of seven or eight children can immediately understand each other ... it simply means that from this age onwards they try to improve upon their methods of interchanging ideas and upon their mutual understanding of one another' (Piaget, 1959, p. 49, 3rd ed.). The contention is that at some age the child comes to realize that there are problems about communicating; he comes to realize that what he says may not be understood, and that what is said to him may not be an unambiguous and clear basis for his own action or understanding. This realization is likely to be accompanied by a knowledge of various ways of improving the situation when communication fails. In this chapter we shall review evidence relevant to developmental changes in the child's conception of the way verbal referential communication works and we offer some suggestions about the consequences of these changes for communicative performance. We shall not be attempting to make either a comprehensive historical appraisal of the extent to which Piaget's writings contribute to the field, or a detailed conceptual analysis of the terms used to discuss the issues.

Piaget's (1926) original definitions and measures of 'egocentric speech' did not lead him to claim that *all* the speech of children between the ages of four and seven could be identified as 'egocentric', although it was to that set of features he paid most attention. He did write later however that in adult conversations 'in the first place each one tries to influence the other; ... the object in view is always to modify the other speaker's conduct or thought. Secondly and just because of this, each one distinguishes between his own point of view and the other man's'. He continues 'Now the child is in some degree capable of all this when still quite young, and "socialized" speech no doubt comes as early as speech itself: when still in its infancy the child shows the greatest skill (moreover an almost unconscious skill) in trying to get what he wants from others' (1959, p. 261, 3rd ed.). That Piaget's interest was caught by the failures to adapt rather than by the successes in doing so cannot be used to infer that his observations were inaccurate or even incomplete. In fact a reading of either the final chapter of *The Language and Thought of the Child* or of his reply to Vygotsky's criticisms (1962) reveals much more qualification and elaboration of these matters than secondary sources are likely to include. It also reveals (in spite of the quotation below on p. 6) a firmness of conviction that the adaptiveness of much natural speech cannot be used to infer a general absence of cognitive egocentrism if symptoms of the latter appear both regularly and predictably (Piaget, 1962, pp. 2–7); in particular, for example, when the situation obliges the child to cope with difficulties or breakdowns in verbal referential communication. And as Menig-Peterson (1975) points out from her experiment, an observer who focused on how the verbal productions of young children shifted across listeners would note the 'appropriate tailoring of their communication', whereas one who attended to children's verbalizations to the naïve listener would notice that the children 'were making a lot of egocentric mistakes' (1975, p. 1018).

To demonstrate apparent adaptiveness in some contexts offers facts to be explained but a demonstration is not an explanation in itself, neither does it account for the regular and predictable failures to adapt in other contexts. These demonstrations of shifts in speech features by very young children as a function of differences in participants and situations have led to a moving away from a concern with 'egocentric speech' and a rejection of Piaget's concept of 'egocentrism', but this movement has occurred by default rather than as a result of valid argumentation invoking alternative explanations.

Systematic variability in the speech of young children has been described in terms of the child having 'implicit' or 'tacit' knowledge or understanding which in turn is treated as grounds for suggesting that he is not egocentric in his thinking. To categorize behaviour as revealing 'tacit understanding' does not either describe or explain that behaviour. Why the operation of the 'implicit knowledge' does not extend to eliminate all the failures to adapt is also left on one side, or dispatched into the undefined 'performance factors' waste paper basket. If we are eventually to construct useful and comprehensive theories they must deal with the total behaviour, embracing both the failures and the successes of children's communicative competence. If Piaget can be accused of neglecting the latter, some of his antagonists can be charged with neglecting the former.

Part of the difficulty seems to stem from a lack of explicitness and consensus about the meanings to be associated with the words 'know' and 'understand'. What are the criterial features of 'knowledge'? What are the similarities and differences between types of knowledge, if those are distinctions to be made? In recent years the North American bias has been towards linguists and psychologists being surprised by the earliness of the appearance of signs of 'implicit' or 'tacit' knowledge, this bias being particularly evident in comments about language development. For example, in an introduction to the subject, taking Chomsky as one point of departure, Cazden wrote (1972, p. 7):

> When we say that a person, either child or adult, knows a set of rules, we don't mean that he knows them in any conscious way. Usually, knowledge refers to something we are aware of knowing, something we could, if we wished, verbalize on demand. But linguistic rules are known only non-consciously, out-of-awareness, as a kind of powerful but implicit, or tacit, knowledge. This is true for adults as well as for children.

Cazden mentions criteria for inferring the presence of such knowledge: we generally use forms appropriately, and when given novel or nonsense words or sentences we will create forms in accordance with rules. Such criteria might cause philosophers to lose sleep or turn in their graves if they distinguish between *knowledge* and *belief* and reserve the former for true belief; you cannot 'know' the plural of 'wug'. Another criterion is that when 'a rule is violated, we have a general sense that something is amiss' (1972, p. 7). And what is 'a general sense'?

Alas, the originators and developers of these ideas have failed to construct definitions of their key concepts in such a way that we can see the similarities and differences between them and then relate them to cognate terms in the associated universe of discourse. Distinctions between knowledge and belief have not been exposed. Kinds of knowledge have not been discussed in terms of manner of representation or other dimensions of quality. Are we discussing action schemes, concrete operational structures, or formal operational structures, to use the Piagetian terminology? Or enactive, iconic, or symbolic modes, if we use Bruner's (1966)? What is 'implicit knowledge'? Does it include activities which are represented enactively through the operation of action schemes, viz. all animate behaviour? Further, does it make sense to claim that for some knowledge at least, we know that we know? Are there kinds of knowledge, e.g. logical, empirical, moral, aesthetic, religious, which are known differently?

We could have been saved from much muddle had more psychologists, linguists, and sociologists taken note of philosophical contributions to this subject, if, for example, they had built upon Ryle's (1949) distinctions between 'belief' and 'knowledge', 'knowing' and 'knowing that you know', and between 'knowing how to' and 'knowing that'. We do not pretend to resolve these issues here. We do no more than mention them and declare the policy we shall adopt in our terminology, noting that the distinctions we made are little more than a temporary expedient for presenting and interpreting data.

Requirements for effective verbal referential communication

The fundamental concern here is with the transmission of propositional knowledge, mediated verbally. The speaker has the task of relaying information to a receiver, in particular he has to select and formulate a message that identifies a referent uniquely for a listener. The listener has to identify and select the referent from an array of possible referents relying upon the message he receives. We wish to describe and explain the beliefs and knowledge that children can bring to bear in coping with and solving such problems, and to describe how their beliefs and knowledge develop.

By using appropriate materials and instructions, the characteristics and composition of which do not in themselves overwhelm the child's psychological capacities and/or exceed his knowledge, we can approach the heart of the matter – does he realize that the message must refer uniquely to the referent? If a child can identify the ambiguity of an utterance as one of the reasons why referential communication can fail, we treat this as indicative of the child knowing about the role of the message in referential communication. This is a conservative criterion. To attribute 'knowing that' to someone who can explicate this knowledge verbally in an unfamiliar context seems to be a safe inference. We reserve the term 'explicit knowledge' for this achievement. If we can subsequently find alternative criteria which permit similar inferences, these can be integrated then. In terms of the initially cited quotation from Piaget the ability to improve or debase messages might be one such alternative (Robinson and Robinson, 1978a). On the other hand adaptability of performance *per se* might be more parsimoniously and accurately explained through other mechanisms. Direct inferences from performance to claims about the child's knowledge about communication are hazardous and need stronger warrants than appeals to experimenters' preferred modes of attribution. We use the term *'imputed know-how'* for these accomplishments.

Muddles about terminology are not the only hazard. Vagueness and indefiniteness also infect the analysis of performance. Piaget in some parts of *The Language and Thought of the Child* and other authors have sometimes omitted to analyze the many possible reasons for successful or unsuccessful communicative performance. For example, Piaget's definition of 'adapted information' is that it is successful. The child actually makes his hearer listen, and contrives to influence him, i.e. to tell him something. This time the child speaks from the point of view of his audience. 'The function of language is ... actually to communicate his thoughts to other people' (1959, p. 19, 3rd. ed.). Here there seems to be no acceptance either of the possibility that the child could fail to communicate successfully despite an awareness of the need to take into account the other's perspective or the possibility that he could succeed by other means. Similarly, in experiments in which children were asked to relay newly-acquired information to another child, Piaget interprets the incoherence of the children's accounts with 'the words spoken are not thought of from the point of view of the person spoken to' (1959, p. 98, 3rd. ed.). But is this because the child fails to realize he should take into account the other's point of view, or merely because in these particular circumstances he cannot? On the other hand, other authors, having demonstrated that three- and four-year-olds may successfully take their listener's needs into account, have not considered whether this success necessarily stems from a knowledge about the processes involved (e.g. Maratsos, 1973; Menig-Peterson, 1975; Shatz and Gelman, 1973); rather they have focused on the behavioural symptoms of egocentrism.

Flavell, Botkin, Fry, Wright and Jarvis (1968) made explicit the need to consider the various possible reasons for failure or success in communication tasks. They suggested that conscious successful performance requires the possession of certain knowledge and skills: *existence*, or knowing that there is such a thing as perspective; *need*, or knowing that an analysis of perspective is called for now; correct *prediction* and analysis of the relevant perspective; *maintenance* of the awareness of the results of this analysis; and *application* of these results to produce an effective message. Breakdown in any of these could be responsible for communication failure. Subsequent writers have also listed component skills. For example, Glucksberg, Krauss and Higgins (1975) list skills which the child must acquire in order to be a competent communicator: the speaker must determine the non-referents from which the referent stimulus must be distinguished, determine which attributes are criterial, formulate a tentative message, evaluate it in terms of whether, from the point of view of the listener, it adequately differentiates the referent from nonreferents, and if necessary formulate a new message to be evaluated in its turn. The listener's task is to decode the message: he has to examine each stimulus and calculate the match between it and the message. If he can make a confident decision about which is the referent, he will make the appropriate response; if he cannot, he will (should) request additional information.

The greatest emphasis in recent work is upon the importance of comparison activity for successful communicative performance, and the young child's weakness in performing the necessary comparisons. We shall return to this point; it is mentioned here to illustrate the move towards analyzing the child's communicative performance in terms of skills which he does or does not display, and away from making interpretations about whether or not the child is egocentric.

Is the Piagetian concept of egocentrism still a useful one? A number of authors have argued that it is not (e.g. Asher, 1978; Shatz, 1978) for reasons which may well be valid, such as the inability of such a general description to cope with variations in performance across different tasks. However, one advantage of initially adopting a Piagetian stance is that it guards against imputing knowledge or understanding unnecessarily. Those who have argued against the usefulness of egocentrism have tended to ignore the distinctions between 'knowing how' and 'knowing that' mentioned above. For example, Shatz (1978) states that 'there are two basic kinds of understanding that are involved in communicative skill: Social understanding and understanding of message content' (p. 3). As evidence that the former is already present among preschoolers she takes the facts that they can maintain smooth social interaction, taking turns in conversation, and that they may make comments on those who violate convention. At what level of communicative performance across how many kinds of adaptation *must* one conclude that the child understands, in the sense of 'knowing about' the need to take into account the listener's point of view? Is there a change of quality or only quantity? Perhaps there is no level which warrants a categorical shift in mode of explanation of his performance, but the issue is worth considering, whatever the eventual conclusion drawn.

One way of tackling this problem is to try to construct a comprehensive and detailed description of the developmental sequence (or sequences) of the child's imputed know-how and explicit assumptions about the communicative process. The data bases from which the descriptions are to be derived are several: (1) aspects of communicative performance itself, (2) judgements about aspects of communication tasks, and (3) comments about how one should proceed in such tasks. All three need to be integrated if we are to chart the child's changing assumptions about the features involved in successful and unsuccessful verbal communication. This approach can be applied to any of the significant factors in the communication process, e.g. the role of the listener in supplying feedback to the speaker, the speaker's responsibility to engage the listener's interest. Here we focus mainly upon one central aspect of the process: the need for the speaker to take into account the listener's information requirements, and in particular the need to identify uniquely the intended referent from the listener's point of view. After we have suggested a sequence of descriptions of the child's imputed know-how and explicit assumptions about these matters, we shall proceed to claim that once his imputed know-how manifests certain qualities we may conclude that the child has the capacity to become aware of the need to take into account the listener's information requirements; it becomes necessary to say that the child 'knows about' the essence of this central aspect of verbal communication. We can then examine the measure of match between the know-how and the corresponding explicit beliefs. Before this argument is elaborated, however, we must review data of the three kinds mentioned and show how they can be used to formulate the relevant descriptions.

Evidence about the child's imputed know-how and explicit knowledge

(1) *Communicative performance itself*

We have already referred to evidence which demonstrates that younger children are prone not to make exhaustive comparisons between the intended referent and other potential referents either when they are formulating messages or when they are reacting to them. Asher and his colleagues (Asher and Oden, 1976; Asher and

Parke, 1975) used a procedure which required the child to identify for an imaginary listener which of a pair of words was underlined, e.g. *ocean*-river; the child was asked to produce a clue that would achieve identification. Younger children (2nd grade) were less likely than older ones to consider the non-referent word (and thereby exclude it) as well as the referent when producing their clues.

Comparable results have been obtained with younger children by Whitehurst and his colleagues. Whitehurst and Sonnenschein (1978a) asked five-year-olds to describe one of a pair of triangles so that the listener could identify it. Pretesting had shown that all the children had the vocabulary necessary to describe the features of the triangles. The children gave informative messages when all that varied over trials was the *value* of the relevant dimension of the referent (which was designated for the child). For example, the referent might always be either the red triangle or the black triangle, with all other differences between the triangles remaining constant over trials. However, the children failed to give informative messages when the *relevant dimension* itself varied over trials; it might be colour, size or pattern. Shatz (1978) argues that the children's success on the easy pairs suggests that they did make comparisons when they could cope with the cognitive workload involved. An alternative possibility is that they merely described what was perceptually most salient, i.e. that which changed over trials, with no understanding of the importance of describing the identifying attribute of the designated triangle (Robinson and Robinson, 1978b).

Very late appearance of comparison activity was found by Tenney and Apthorp (reported in Whitehurst and Sonnenschein, 1978b) who asked children to describe to a listener the dress of one of two dolls. The dolls were in different houses. The authors found that it was not until the age of 11 that children looked in both houses when they were producing their messages.

Whereas Asher and Oden (1976) assumed that the children's failure to make comparisons was due to their inability to do so, and argued for weakness in comparison skills as an alternative explanation to egocentrism for poor communicative performance, Whitehurst and Sonnenschein (1978b) have subsequently demonstrated that this is too simple a view. Younger children can perform the comparisons when given certain instructions. These authors again used pairs of triangles one of which was designated for the child to describe for a listener. Five-year-old children were either told 'Tell me about the triangle with the star above it so that I will know which triangle you are talking about' or 'Tell me how the triangle with the star above it looks different from the other triangle'. As in the complex condition of their earlier experiment, the relevant dimension varied over trials; it could be colour, size or pattern. The children who were asked to describe differences gave 73% informative messages, whereas those who were asked to describe the triangle for the listener gave only 50%. Those in the former group gave more messages containing only the minimum necessary information; the informative messages of those in the latter group were more likely to contain redundant information.

In a subsequent experiment Whitehurst and Sonnenschein (1978b) attempted to train children to describe differences. The most effective method was found to be to give the child the 'communication' instructions used above, 'Tell me so I know which one', followed by feedback about whether or not he had described differences: 'That's good; you told me how the triangle with the star above it was different from the other', or 'That's wrong; you did not tell me how the triangle with the star above it was different from the other'. The children receiving this treatment achieved a success rate of 83% informative messages. Three other treatments were less successful: (1) giving communication instructions with advice to tell about differences, whether or not they also received feedback about whether they had described differences, (2) giving communication instructions with only a non-commital nod or 'OK' as feedback, and (3) giving communication instructions followed by feedback about whether or not they had described it so the listener knew which one. Ignoring the details of the results, it is clear that telling children to describe differences increases their rate of production of informative messages. One could conclude that prior to the experiment the children did not know that communicating effectively requires them to identify the referent uniquely.

The young child's performance as a listener is also consistent with the view that he does not make comparisons when interpreting messages. Ambiguity in messages would not be detected by a child who was failing to make comparisons between possible referents. Lloyd and Paulidis are reported by Whitehurst and Sonnenschein (1978b) as having looked at comparison activity directly by examining child-listeners' eye movements. The younger children, unlike the older ones, showed no visual comparison of the set of potential referents. Clearly at some stage we need to conduct experiments which allow us to make stronger inferences about comparison activity than can be obtained from performance errors and accounts. It is now possible to construct apparatus that will record fine eye movements and if such could be incorporated into appropriate investigations, we should be able to find out whether or not children sample the array. While the presence of apparently systematic eye-movements does not necessarily mean that exhaustive comparison activity is taking place inside the head, the absence of such movements would allow the obverse conclusion.

Less direct evidence comes from the finding of age-related increases in question-asking by child listeners in response to ambiguous messages. Alvy (1968) found that six-year-old pairs of children made fewer requests for clarification than older pairs. Cosgrove and Patterson (1977) found that requestng clarification of an adult speaker was much less common among preschool (four-year-olds) and kindergarten children (six-year-olds) than among older ones (eight- and ten-year-olds). Ironsmith and Whitehurst (1978) obtained similar results. Cosgrove and Patterson (1977) went on to provide children with a 'plan' for effective listening which emphasized the importance of asking for more information if the message was inadequate. On a posttest, those who had received the plan (except the preschoolers) asked more questions and made more correct responses than those who had not.

Patterson, Massad and Cosgrove (1978) attempted to find out whether the children's problem was in knowing that they should make comparisons in order to evaluate the message, or in knowing what to do having identified the message as inadequate. They found that, as before, telling children to ask for more information if the message was ambiguous (action plan) was effective in improving the children's question-asking behaviour and their number of correct responses, whereas giving them a comparison plan was not. They concluded that the children spontaneously made comparisons upon receiving a message, but did not know what to do having identified the inadequacy of the message. This may be the case; however, the 'comparison plan' emphasized to the child that he should '... try to figure out whether you know enough ...' Possibly a plan which made it clearer that the child should see whether the message referred to more than one item would be more effective.

From this evidence about communicative performance we might conclude that we cannot impute to younger children (four- and five-year-olds in these experiments) the know-how that a message must identify the intended referent uniquely.

(2) *Judgements about aspects of communication tasks*

Absence of comparison activity has also been found in the young child's evaluations of messages. In addition, it has been found that good messages are more accurately judged than ambiguous ones. Asher (1976) found that younger (second-grade) children were less successful than older ones at identifying adequate and inadequate clues in the word pair game, whether or not the messages were their own or those of another child. At ages up to sixth grade adequate messages were more accurately judged than inadequate ones. Bearison and Levey (1977) asked children from kindergarten to fourth grade to judge whether questions about sentences which had been read out were 'good' or 'bad'. The adequate questions were readily judged as 'good', but the younger children were less able than older ones at judging inadequate ones as 'bad'. Response preferences for 'good' were not eliminated as a possible contributing factor. Patterson, O'Brien, Carter, Kister and Kotsonis (referred to by Patterson and Kister, 1978) gave children from kindergarten to fourth grade messages which referred to one, two, four or eight potential referents. The youngest children judged all the messages to be adequate (the child was asked whether he could identify the referent or whether he needed another clue); the older children were more likely to spot the inadequacy the greater the number of potential referents.

Markman (1977) presented first to third grade children (six-, seven-, and eight-year-olds) with inadequate instructions on how to perform a trick or play a game, and assessed whether they recognized the inadequacy by asking a sequence of ten questions which asked more and more explicitly whether anything had been omitted. First graders (six-year-olds) tended only to become aware of the inadequacy when they attempted to carry out the instructions or saw them demonstrated. Markman concluded that 'The children appear to be processing material at a relatively superficial level, not really attempting to execute the instructions mentally or determine the relationship between the instructions and the goal. As a consequence, they are left unaware of the inadequacy of the instructions.' (p. 991). Presumably one aspect of active processing of instructions would be to make comparisons between the message and various possible realizations of it.

From these results, the conclusion holds for explicit knowledge, as for imputed know-how, that the young child does not realize the importance of unique identification of the referent; although the evaluation data give no indication of whether the children were capable of performing the comparisons. In addition one might propose that the young child assumes that messages are good (rather than bad or having no conception of good or bad messages).

In a series of experiments we have obtained results which are largely consistent with these two descriptions and which allow us to elaborate this account of the child's explicit assumptions about communication. Most of our data consist of children's judgements about messages and about the locus of responsibility for communicative success or failure. We have also related these judgements to aspects of the child's communicative performance.

In our standard procedure, child and experimenter sit on either side of an opaque screen; each has an identical set of drawings. Sometimes the child observes a game instead of participating. Players take turns to be the speaker, whose initially stated task is to describe one of his drawings so that the listener can pick the matching one from his set. The same drawing may be chosen more than once. The drawings we have used are such that children have the vocabulary to describe them, and the ability to identify differences between them, but they often do not describe uniquely identifying attributes. We have distinguished between materials in which listener and speaker will agree on the reference of a message, and those in which they may not (e.g. with inkblots a speaker may produce an idiosyncratic description). It is possible therefore to separate two potential problems for the child. Does he know that a message should identify the referent uniquely? Does he know that a message which identifies the referent uniquely for himself may not do so for his listener? In most of our work we have used materials for which there is no disagreement about labelling.

During the course of our game, the child on his turns as speaker usually gives an ambiguous (too general) message spontaneously; on these occasions the experimenter as listener will choose wrongly. On some of her turns as speaker, the experimenter deliberately gives ambiguous messages, which refer to two cards rather than one, and whichever card the child chooses the experimenter shows that she had chosen the other. Following these communication failures, the child is asked a standard sequence of questions, the 'whose fault?' sequence: 'We went wrong that time, we got different cards. Whose fault was that? Mine? Yours? Why? Did I/you tell you/me properly which one to pick? (If the child says "No": What should I/you have said?) Whose fault was it we went wrong? Why?'

The responses fall into four categories: *Listener-blamers* judge that it was the listener's fault (whether that be child or experimenter) because it was he who chose the wrong card, judge that the speaker did tell properly although the message referred both to the speaker's chosen card and the listener's, and again repeat that it was the listener's fault. *Lower-intermediates* judge that it was the listener's fault because he chose wrongly, judge that the speaker did not tell properly and identify at least one attribute missing from the message, and again judge that the fault was the listener's. Over a number of judgements about communication failures the child continues to blame only the listener; he may not judge all the ambiguous messages to be inadequate. *Higher-intermediates* judge that it was the listener's fault because he chose wrongly, judge that the speaker did not tell properly and give an adequate reason, and then judge that the speaker was at fault because he did not tell properly. Over a number of judgements about communication failure, the child may cease to place the initial blame on the listener. *Speaker-blamers* judge that it was the speaker's fault because his message was inadequate, judge that the speaker did not tell properly and give an adequate reason, and judge again that the speaker was at fault.

We have found a strong relation between age and category of blame, with listener-blaming being common among five-year-olds and speaker-blaming becoming common by the age of seven (Robinson and Robinson, 1976a and b). It should be added that most of our samples of children have been drawn from predominantly middle class areas and that, with only very few exceptions, the children have entered into the spirit of the game that we have created. Experimenters have been people at ease with young children and have conducted the interrogations with light-hearted efficiency, minimizing in every way the interfering and depressing features of interviewing so vividly portrayed by Labov (1969). We were in contact with our children and they with us. Given that these conditions were achieved the comments of the children represent their best efforts.

In terms of understanding about referential verbal communication, speaker-blamers reveal explicit knowledge of the need to take into account the listener's information requirements. Higher-intermediates also reveal explicit knowledge, but appear to need to be reminded of this; the first interrogatory sequence is sufficient to enable them to realize that this communication situation involves this consideration. We discuss lower-intermediates below. We have no reason to assert that listener-blamers command explicit knowledge, the reverse in fact appears to be true. Neither have we grounds for attributing to them an implicit knowledge of the need to identify referents uniquely.

In our first experiments we also identified a category of 'experimenter-blamers' who blamed the speaker when they were the listener, but the listener when they were the speaker. Given their age and status within the sample we originally interpreted this result as evidence that the child gives the more advanced judgement when he is in the listener rather than the speaker role, and suggested that learning about communication may take place in the listener role (Robinson and Robinson, 1976a and b). However, it now appears that a different interpretation is more likely to be true. In the main experiment in which we obtained experimenter-blamers, the materials were photographs of inkblots, and with these young children tend to produce idiosyncratic descriptions. A child listener to such a description may not agree that the message fits the intended referent at all, let alone uniquely; if so, then from the child listener's point of view the message would be what we have described as inappropriate. We have also found that children who judge too general messages to be adequate may nevertheless judge inappropriate messages to be inadequate on the grounds that they do not describe the intended referent (Robinson and Robinson, 1977b). That is, a child who apparently does not know that a message should describe the intended referent *uniquely* may nevertheless know that it should describe the intended referent. It appears, then, that when a child is listening to messages about inkblots, some of the messages may from his point of view be inappropriate and therefore easier to judge inadequate (and blame the speaker for failure) than those judged in the speaker role which at worst could be seen by him as ambiguous. We have as yet no further evidence about learning in the listener as opposed to the speaker role or *vice versa*.

It is clear from the content of the four categories listed above that children may judge ambiguous messages to be inadequate without necessarily seeing the speaker as responsible for failure. We argued that in order to blame the speaker the child must, as well as conceiving of the inadequacy of ambiguous messages, be able to handle distal (as opposed to just proximal) causes. Evidence that the handling of distal causes is a stumbling block for lower-intermediates came from a study in which children were presented with picture stories in which occurred either a communication failure or an accident for which either a proximal or a distal cause could be blamed. For instance, Steven comes home from a bicycle ride and asks his mother for a drink. In one story he is given an orange drink but really wanted a green drink (communication failure); in the matching one his mother brings him a green drink but trips over his bike which he has left across the doorway and spills the drink (accident). Is the non-receipt of the orange drink attributed to the mother (proximal) or the boy (distal)? There was a close relationship between the cause blamed (proximal or distal) in the two types of story. Those categorized as lower-intermediates on the basis of their judgements about the communication failures, had difficulty with distal causes in the accident stories (Robinson and Robinson, 1978b).

In our subsequent work, we have concentrated upon investigating the development of understanding about message inadequacy rather than role blaming, although in work mentioned below we found it to be blame judgements rather than adequacy judgements which were more closely related to aspects of communicative performance (Robinson and Robinson, 1978b). Along with other authors (Asher, Whitehurst, Patterson and others) we have observed the young child's failure to make comparisons between the intended and unintended referents. Asher and Oden (1976) saw weak comparison activity as an alternative to 'egocentrism' as an explanation of poor communicative performance. An alternative possibility is that the young child fails to make the necessary comparisons *because* he does not know that a message should refer uniquely to whatever the speaker has in mind; this in turn could itself be interpreted as a symptom of egocentrism. Consistent with our interpretation is evidence that young children can perform the necessary comparisons in a non-communication situation even though they fail to perform them in the communication evaluation game. In order to judge an ambiguous message to be inadequate, the young child has to compare the intended referent with the listener's incorrect choice, observe that the message fits both equally well, and see the relevance of that for the adequacy judgement. We devised a task which required the same comparisons to be made (Robinson and Robinson, 1978c). The experimenter presented a sequence of pairs of cards equivalent to those used for the message adequacy judgements, and turned over one, the other, or both. The child was asked to complete the sentence 'I've turned over all the cards with ...' That is, the child had to identify what was common to both cards and what was unique to each. Children could be successful in this task while nevertheless judging ambiguous messages to be adequate; there was none who failed the task while judging ambiguous messages to be inadequate. It appeared, then, that the child's problem was not in performing the comparisons but in seeing the relevance of performing them in a communication setting. This is quite consistent with Whitehurst's results summarized above.

It appears then that the five-year-old child as assessed by his explicit knowledge may be described as knowing that a message should refer to the intended referent but he does not know that it should identify it uniquely. He does not know that an ambiguous message can cause communication failure. What does he know about the causes of successful communication? As mentioned above Bearison and Levey

(1977) found that children were better at identifying good messages as good than bad ones as bad. The first assumption of the children was that messages were good. We have found that some of our listener-blamers mentioned the message when answering 'How did we get it right?' (Robinson and Robinson, 1977a). Moreover, some of them were more likely to do so when the message was in fact good than when it was ambiguous. They appeared to recognize good messages as such when communication was successful, even though they could not identify ambiguous messages as inadequate or as responsible for communication failure. None of the children at this level of development had any difficulty in blaming the listener when the message was in fact good but the listener chose wrongly; it was older children, who judged ambiguous messages to be responsible for communication failure, who tried to find reasons for the failure in the good message. It would seem to be inaccurate to describe the five-year-old as having no idea that messages can be adequate or inadequate, no idea about the role of the message in communication success or failure. He apparently assumes that good messages are responsible for successful communication; his problem is in coming to realize that there are bad messages and in learning what their characteristics are. He may know that a message which does not even refer to the intended referent (from his point of view) can be responsible for communication failure (though some of our children apparently did not even know this).

(3) *Comments about how one should proceed in a communication task*

We have found a strong association between children's ascriptions of blame for communication failure and their answers to 'How would we make sure we got it right next time?' Whereas 83.3% of children who blamed the speaker for failure mentioned the message only 3.7% of those who blamed the listener for failure did this. These children suggested that the listener should try harder, or merely stated that the players would 'get it right' (Robinson and Robinson, 1978b).

Interpretation of evidence concerning imputed know-how and explicit knowledge

From the evidence presented about children's judgements and comments about communication, we can formulate tentatively the following sequence of descriptions of the child's explicit knowledge about the processes involved in communication:
1. An early stage which we have not adequately investigated because the child is too young to respond to our questioning procedures.
2. The child treats all messages as though they are adequate if from his point of view they refer to whatever was intended by the speaker. The child judges that a message may be responsible for communicative success; in this respect he may

discriminate between good and ambiguous messages. However, he judges the listener to be responsible for communication failure when the message is ambiguous. He judges messages to be inadequate and blames the speaker only when the message is inappropriate.

3. The child realizes that for a message to be adequate it must refer uniquely to whatever the speaker intended from the listener's point of view. We have as yet no evidence of a separation of these two components of unique reference and point of view, although further investigation might demonstrate the existence of children who realize the importance of unique reference without recognizing the possibility of different interpretations of a particular message, or of children who recognize the latter but not the former (Robinson and Robinson, 1978c). The child judges ambiguous messages to be inadequate; he judges idiosyncratic messages to be inadequate; he may nevertheless blame the listener for failure unless he can already handle distal causes. Once he does begin to blame the speaker, he may attempt to justify such an allocation of blame whenever there is communication failure, even if the listener could more appropriately be blamed.

4. The child sees the communicative process as an interaction between speaker and listener in which there is joint responsibility for achieving understanding. We have as yet no firm evidence about this stage, though piloting suggests that from the age of about nine or ten the child may begin to consider it inappropriate to blame only the speaker for failure if the listener gave no indication of non-understanding. Before this stage is reached, the child can consider each role separately, but not the coordination of the two.

This sequence of descriptions is to be taken as a basis for further experimentation and discussion rather than as a confident and unique interpretation of the evidence.

It is in general consistent with the descriptions of the child's imputed know-how constructed from the evidence about the child's communicative performance: children of about the age when they are at our second stage apparently do not make exhaustive comparisons in communicative performance. We know that children who would still be at the first stage in our sequence are capable of taking listener characteristics such as age or sightedness into account (Maratsos, 1973; Shatz and Gelman, 1973) and in this respect they cannot be described as behaving only from their own point of view. In what respects does the child's explicit knowledge provide an under-estimate of his understanding about communication? As mentioned earlier, verbal comment about occurrences in experimental settings is likely to provide a strict criterion for the child's understanding. We shall, however, argue that imputed know-how and explicit knowledge about communication present a consistent account of development. We suggest that once the child realizes the importance of comparison activity for successful speaking and successful listening, his knowledge about this aspect of communication must become explicit and not remain as know-how realized only through certain forms of action. Three authors have made comments relevant to this position:

Flavell (1977) states that 'Much of what constitutes metacognitive development may be the growing ability and disposition to think about 'messages', in the broad sense, and about the cognitive experiences these messages may engender in people. ... (The young child) does not have the metacognition that the message as it stands justifies only an incomplete and tentative interpretation on his part. ... The young child converts messages into cognitive representations and vice-versa, but both the messages and the representations are largely invisible to him.' (pp. 32–33).

Markman (1978) suggests that 'active attempts to comprehend ... require some meta-cognitive knowledge ... much information about one's comprehension is a by-product of active attempts to understand and not just of attempts to monitor' (p. 21).

Shatz (1978) after pointing out that in a standard referential communication task a comparison process is necessary, states that 'While the analyses of individual items may become automatic, the comparison process is much less likely to do so. How often, after all, does one describe an item as a function of the *same* set of field items? Thus, the critical feature comparison process is typically confined to the conscious level.' (p. 33). Shatz goes on to argue that the amount of cognitive effort required for the initial analyses of the items will determine whether or not the child has the additional resources available to go on to the critical feature analysis.

The suggestion is, then, that there is an association between making comparisons, being 'active' in one's attempt to understand or be understood, and being aware or being capable of becoming aware of one's activity. If the child manifests apparent know-how of the necessity to make comparisons, evidenced by his performance as a speaker or a listener, then he must also behave in an active way towards the materials he is dealing with, and must be capable of becoming aware of what the problems are. That is not to say that he must be aware of what he is doing at the time of making comparisons; rather that he should be able to comment upon events after they have happened, e.g. explain why communication succeeded or failed.

If this argument is valid, we should not expect to find children whose communicative performance suggests that they know that messages should refer uniquely to the intended referent, but whose judgements or comments about communication suggests that they do not. We may find children who show knowledge of the importance of comparison activity in their judgements or comments but not in their communicative performance, since the child may fail to perform correctly the comparisons necessary for a particular task while nevertheless realizing (at the time or in retrospect) what he should have done.

We have begun to accumulate some experimental evidence relevant to this prediction:

1. In a study of real-life mother–child interaction (Robinson and Robinson, 1979) we found evidence of significant covariation between early development of speaker-blaming in an experimental situation and previous ways of the child handling communication failures in the home. Children who were speaker-blaming by the age of six were more likely than those who were still listener-blamers at that age to take the initiative during their preschool years in registering failures of communication; only these children used phrases such as 'I don't understand' or 'I don't know what you mean'. While these appeared only rarely in the transcripts of those who by the age of six were speaker-blamers, they did not occur at all in those of those who at six were still listener-blamers.

2. What kinds of questions do children ask when they are listeners receiving an inadequate message? In a training experiment described below (Robinson and Robinson, 1979) types of questions differed across categories of children. Those who were speaker-blamers at the outset of the experiment asked only open questions, such as 'What else?' or 'What colour?'; children in the other blame categories asked disjunctive or closed questions 'Has it got long or short sleeves?', 'Is it blue?'. No child who was still a listener-blamer at the end of the experiment asked an open questions, whereas six of the ten who were speaker-blamers at the outset had asked at least one.

3. Can children control the adequacy of their messages? Can they give 'easier' messages which reduce ambiguity and 'harder' messages which increase the number of possible referents? We obtained a base line establishing children's average ambiguity of messages and then asked them to make it harder for the listener to choose. Of 18 listener-blamers only two managed to give more ambiguous messages, whereas 30 of the 40 speaker-blamers did so. There was a corresponding significant differentiation for 'easy' messages (Robinson and Robinson, 1978a).

4. In an experiment (Robinson and Robinson, 1978b) where the children began by giving messages about a card which was the only up-turned one in an array there were no differences in the quality of the messages of speaker- and listener-blamers. Once all cards were visible the speaker-blamers gave more adequate messages than the listener-blamers, presumably because they made more comparisons between the intended referent and the other cards.

5. We are beginning to look more systematically at relations between understanding and communicative performance in a context where children have to tell the experimenter how to construct simple models of cars or houses from components of Lego kits. Speaker-blamers and listener-blamers are equally adept in the specificity of their reference to the individual components. However, with respect to the positioning of pieces in relation to each other, speaker-blamers give more information than their listener-blaming peers.

The general tenor of these results is not particularly surprising, but the facts might have been different and it will probably be through a detailed examination of what happens at the transition points of development across a variety of task requirements that we will be able to build up a sufficiently comprehensive data-base for any proposed explanation to have a reasonably secure foundation. With the evidence so far obtained we can say that if children can say what they should do when formulating messages, then their performance generally reflects there imperatives.

The evidence and arguments presented in the preceding sections lead us to describe the young child as lacking in understanding about at least one central aspect of the communicative process: the need for the speaker to identify the intended referent uniquely from the listener's point of view. How does he acquire this understanding? Presumably certain qualities of his verbal interactions with adults and other children are relevant to development. In this section we shall begin to try and identify what these might be.

Development of explicit knowledge about communication

If the young child initially assumes that his communications will be successful, this could be because from his point of view they usually are. While the child is himself an inexpert speaker, he will frequently be interacting with an expert listener, namely an adult who is familiar with the range of comments the child is likely to make and who is able to make acceptable interpretations of messages with little information content. Even if the listener does not in fact understand the young child's message, he may register his nonunderstanding in such a way that the young child does not recognize that there has been communication failure. Evidence relevant to these comments will be summarized below. Some of the evidence and interpretations have appeared in greater detail elsewhere (Robinson, 1978).

In an analysis of adult–child verbal interaction data collected by Clough (1971) and Cambourne (1971) in Australian schools, preschools and homes, we found verbal signalling of misunderstandings and nonunderstandings to be rare. Only about 2% of adult's utterances which were part of an exchange appeared to be inadequate from the child's point of view, and about 8% of children's utterances from the adult point of view. It appeared that adults either do understand most of what children are saying to them or succeed in continuing an exchange despite incomplete understanding. If they do understand this could be because they can predict much of what the child is likely to say as much as because the children are expert communicators. Whatever the reason, the young child's experience of communication failure seems to be limited. No wonder, then, that he has to learn about its extent and the reasons for it.

His learning about it is probably slower than it need be because of the way adults deal with misunderstandings and nonunderstandings. From the Clough and

Cambourne data, we found that by far the most common way for adults to deal with children's inadequate messages was to request a repetition ('what?') or to ask a question to draw from the child the missing information. It was very rare for adults to make explicit that there had been a misunderstanding. Whereas these ways of dealing with inadequate messages would inform an adult that there had been communication failure, they appear not to be interpreted in this way by young children. We devised an experiment in which a series of cardboard cutout children had lost an article of clothing and asked their imaginary Mums for help: 'Mum, have you seen my cardigan please?' The Mums gave different responses, ranging from 'Which one?' to 'You've got two cardigans, I don't know which one you mean. You should tell me which one'. The child subject was asked whether the Mum knew just what the cardboard child wanted, and whether that child had said enough about what he/she wanted. When the Mum asked 'Which one?' or verbalized a correct guess 'Do you mean the red one?', many children thought she had understood. It was easier for them to recognize nonunderstanding when she guessed incorrectly or when she made explicit that she did not know what was wanted. That is, it appeared that the common adult way of dealing with children's inadequate messages, although effective in enabling understanding to be reached, often does not inform the child that there has been a problem. He is allowed to assume that communication was successful.

In a subsequent experiment, we demonstrated that telling the child precisely what was missing from his messages helped him both to improve his subsequent messages and to increase his understanding about message inadequacy and its role in causing communication failure (at least in the short term; we did not have a delayed post-test). In this experiment the child chose clothes for a cardboard doll to wear. There were eight versions of each of six types of garment. The child's task was to choose one of each type and describe it so that the experimenter could dress her doll in the same way. Each child received one of three types of feedback following the giving of an inadequate description: for one third of the children she made a guess, for one third she said 'Which one?', waited for a response from the child and then chose as best she could; for the remaining children she told them what her problem was, e.g. 'Well I've got four like that. I don't know whether it's got long sleeves or short   sleeves, and I don't know whether it's got stripes or checks'. When the child had supplied the missing information, the experimenter chose as best she could. This type of feedback was continued over six trials. We found that the explicit feedback helped the children who were listener-blamers at the outset in two ways: first, they gave better initial descriptions (*before* the feedback was given in any one trial) than those in the other two groups, and second, they were more likely than the others to have advanced out of the listener-blaming category by the end of the experiment.

Recent work by other authors has also been successful in improving children's communicative performance: Whitehurst and Sonnenschein, 1978b; Cosgrove and Patterson, 1977; Patterson, Massad and Cosgrove, 1978; Asher and Wigfield, 1978. This is in contrast to earlier training studies (Fry, 1966, 1969; Shantz and Wilson, 1972), which were relatively unsuccessful. It appears that workers in the field have now hit upon the relevant factor: the child must be enabled to see the importance of comparison activity for the production of good messages or for the understanding of other's messages.

However, none of this work demonstrates how children in fact come to learn about communication in their normal development. We have been fortunate enough to have available data collected under the direction of Wells which enabled us to begin to tackle·this problem (Robinson and Robinson, 1979). The Wells' team recorded mother–child interaction between the ages of 15 months and five years; we analyzed a sub-sample of these data: 36 children and their mothers, beginning when the child was two years old. We coded the ways in which mothers dealt with nonunderstandings and misunderstandings and divided the 11 ways into two categories: those in which the mother explicitly informed the child that there had been a communication failure ('I don't know what you're on about' 'I don't know what you mean') and those in which this information remained implicit: the mother said 'Eh?', 'Pardon?', made a guess or asked a question to extract the missing information. We tested 36 children at the age of six years using our 'whose fault' technique to assess their understanding of message inadequacy and its role in causing communication failure. We were interested in the relationship between mothers' ways of dealing with communication failure during the preschool years, and children's level of understanding about these aspects of communication. The results were clearcut: all those (N = 16) whose mothers had explicitly informed them about communication failure were in the higher-intermediate or speaker-blaming categories; none of those (N = 10) in the lower-intermediate or listener-blaming categories had mothers who gave this explicit information. We could identify no other differences between the mothers who did and did not give explicit information: they did not differ in the frequency of use of implicit ways of dealing with communication failure; social class and level of their children's language development (as measured by mean length of utterance – MLU) appeared not to be relevant. There were ten children in the higher-intermediate and speaker-blaming categories whose mothers did not according to the transcripts explicitly inform them about communication failure. Possibly they did so but not when they were being recorded; possibly the children received this information from sources outside the home; possibly they received other treatment which was equally effective in advancing their level of understanding about communication, though we could not identify from the transcripts what this might have been.

We have, then, evidence from experimental and observational sources consistent with the view that giving the child explicit information about communication failure helps him to understand. We do not know whether this information is necessary. We assume it is not sufficient: as already mentioned the child must be able to make the necessary comparisons and be able to handle distal causes; presumably there are other more basic cognitive requirements. However, it is possible that lack of information about the communicative process is the five-year-old's immediate problem, rather than a cognitive incapacity to comprehend the reasons for successful or unsuccessful communication.

So far, we have assumed that the child learns from failures in communication while in the speaking role. That failure rather than success provides the context for learning seems probable since failure (especially when failure is coded as such by the child) is the exceptional event: presumably it is this which he will first try to explain against a background of assumed success. Learning in the speaking role, i.e. learning from feedback by the listener, may well be supplemented by learning in the listening role, however. There is a body of work demonstrating age-related differences in listener behaviour, some of which has been mentioned: asking of questions (Cosgrove and Patterson, 1977); awareness of nonunderstanding (Markman, 1977); adequacy judgements (Patterson and Kister, 1978; Robinson and Robinson, all references). It may well be that there are opportunities for learning about message inadequacy and its part in causing communication failure especially associated with the listener role. However, researchers have yet to conjecture and check what these might be.

Summary and conclusions

It is probably unnecessary to apologise for the contemporary weakness of the theoretical framework and data base in the area under review; only a few people have as yet turned their attention to the issues involved and they have done so only in the last few years. In several important respects the beginnings are promising, and a critical evaluation can be used to point to fears and hopes for the future rather than to wander helplessly through a morass of apparently irreconcilable results. Some regrets can be expressed, some warnings offered, but these can be made in a spirit of guarded optimism.

One reassuring feature of the work is that largely independent research workers scattered across the United States and Europe are producing similar results with different techniques and procedures. For example, Asher, Patterson, Robinson and Whitehurst each find that children 'cope' with good messages before bad ones, be that coping a matter of giving appropriate answers, asking questions, evaluating messages or ascribing responsibility for success and failure. Similarly Patterson, Robinson and Whitehurst have each been able to devise techniques that enable children to improve their messages, evaluations of messages, or both. Furthermore they agree that precise explicit instructions that focus directly on the reasons for the child's incompetence are the most facilitative of the interventions so far tried. Each also finds that such improvements are easy to achieve with some children at least; this ease is an important consideration for the kind of explanation to be offered for the initial incompetence. It precludes an appeal to a deep seated general cognitive egocentrism. Identity of results and potential coherence of data extant are not always achieved in child development. Whether this is because investigators are becoming wiser experimenters in the late 1970s or simply because the data are few has yet to emerge.

Perhaps we are becoming wiser and more modest. Two related features of the work reviewed can be mentioned which contrast with studies of child language development in the late 1960s and early 1970s. We are not using highly detailed individual case studies to erect universal theories. Attention to detail is important, but we have to achieve the correct measure of fineness; we can use measures too fine or too gross. Small sets of utterances of a child taken on perhaps a single particular day were subjected to very fine syntactic analyses without checks on reliability and stability of the data and with little appreciation that one was dealing with a creature that was capable of variability and change. The analysis was too fine in these respects. In others it was too limited.

Prosodic features were not incorporated within the syntactic framework. That children spoke to some purpose (pragmatics) when communicating meanings (semantics) was left entirely outside the parameters of consideration. It was not until 1970 that Bloom's contribution began to remove some semantic blinkers and not until 1975 that Halliday asserted the primacy of function in the earliest speech of children. Both, however, were still relying on very small numbers of children for their conclusions.

Work on verbal referential communication seems to be avoiding these problems. Sample sizes incorporate at least a two digit number of children in each treatment or contrast group, giving, it is hoped, some degree of reliability and stability to the results. The tasks involve the children listening or speaking to some purpose; in that speech the lexis and grammar are the servants of function, but the utterances are treated as integrated wholes. It is hoped that this means that analysis proceeds at an appropriate level at a degree of fineness which is commensurate with the acts of communication involved. Interpretations of the data are modest and checked.

For example, Markman (1977) argued that one reason why younger children fail to notice inadequacy of instructions lies in their failure to rehearse mentally the sequences involved; it was not until they began to perform the actions that they found they reached choice points where they did not know what to do. Markman checked and supported this hypothesis with a second experiment. Robinson and Robinson (1978b) discovered the existence of children who said in the communication failure situation that it was the listener's fault but that the listener was not told properly. They reasoned that understanding about causes acting distally rather than proximally may be necessary for an appreciation of the link between message inadequacy and the speaker; a subsequent experimental analysis corroborated this suggestion (Robinson and Robinson, 1978b). Patterson and Whitehurst have similarly offered possible reasons for results obtained and have not left these dangling as logically possible explanations. They have probed their plausibility empirically, step by step. Because conjectures have been tested the data and their explanations are growing in step with each other. The field is not replete with bare facts. Neither has theory escalated in generality and abstraction and lost touch with the precise problems in view. If this dialectical balance is maintained, issues will not be raised to an untestable level of abstraction. Neither are we so likely to become embroiled in sterile arguments about meanings of key concepts such as understanding or knowing. While these can be kept in touch with the behaviour to which they are applied (or from which they are withheld) we can retain a clear perception of what is being labelled even if we are individually worried about that label. As long as we know what is being discussed, idiosyncratic preferences for meanings of words should not lead to more than momentary misunderstandings.

The explanations currently offered to account for the data are little more than descriptions. Markman, Patterson, the Robinsons and Whitehurst cannot be said to have produced a theory. Asher's hypotheses about weakness of comparison activity in young children were derived from an S-R type framework initiated by Rosenberg and Cohen (1966), but since the evidence is failing to offer general support for the hypotheses, this potentially constructive effort would appear to be wrong not in conception but as a matter of fact. Robinson and Robinson (1979) are still prepared to use 'egocentrism' in a Piagetian sense, not so much as a final explanation for the communicative behaviour of younger children, but as at least a temporary way of marking apparent characteristics of some of their speech. If the speech can be shown to have such features only because no one has made clear to children what needs to be done in a situation to improve communicative efficiency and that such instruction quickly changes their behaviour, then the label 'egocentrism' can be swiftly dropped. We therefore view egocentrism as a valuable residual explanatory concept to invoke in the absence of better explanations. Markman, Patterson and Whitehurst do not use the term.

The Piagetian notions of 'decentration' and 'general cognitive egocentrism' seem to us to provide an excellent point of departure for relevant studies. Our developmental study of mother–child interaction in relation to the onset of speaker-blaming and judgements of message inadequacy suggest that Piaget was right in saying that the younger child does not know what the requirements of effective referential communication are, but wrong in assuming that the immediate problem is cognitively-based rather than socially determined.

One way ahead is therefore to seek for alternative explanations as to why children have not yet learned what they could learn and to examine these in relation to relatively specific 'knowings how to' and 'knowings that' in relatively specific contexts. Provided that we examine problems imaginatively at a fine enough level of detail, we should be able to construct both a solid data base and explanations to go with this. If cross-sectional studies are linked with longitudinal investigations, and experimentally-founded results are checked against development in real life, we shall succeed in advancing knowledge in this area.

References

ALVY, K. T. (1968) 'Relation of age to children's egocentric and co-operative communication'. *Journal of Genetic Psychology*, **12**, 275–286.

ASHER, S. R. (1976) 'Children's ability to appraise their own and another person's communication performance'. *Developmental Psychology*, **12**, 24–32.

ASHER, S. R. (1978) 'Referential communication'. In WHITEHURST, G. J. and ZIMMERMAN, B. J. (Eds.) *The Functions of Language and Cognition*. New York: Academic Press.

ASHER, S. R. and ODEN, S. L. (1976) 'Children's failure to communicate: an assessment of comparison and egocentrism explanations'. *Developmental Psychology*, **12**, 132–139.

ASHER, S. R. and PARKE, R. D. (1975) 'Influence of sampling and comparison processes on the development of communication effectiveness'. *Journal of Educational Psychology*, **67**, 64–75.

ASHER, S. R. and WIGFIELD, A. (1978) 'Training referential communication skills'. Paper presented at conference on Children's Oral Communication Skills, University of Wisconsin.

BEARISON, D. J. and LEVEY, L. M. (1977) 'Children's comprehension of referential communication: decoding ambiguous messages'. *Child Development*, **48**, 716–720.

BLOOM, L. (1970) *Language development*. Boston, Mass.: The MIT Press.

BRUNER, J. S., OLVER, R. R. and GREENFIELD, P. M. (1966) *Studies in Cognitive Growth*. New York: Wiley.

CAMBOURNE, B. L. (1971) 'A Naturalistic Study of Language Performance in Grade I Rural and Urban School Children'. Unpublished doctoral dissertation, James Cook University, Queensland.

CAZDEN, C. B. (1972) *Child Language and Education*. New York: Holt.

CLOUGH, J. R. (1971) 'An Experimental Investigation of the Effects of a Cognitive Training Programme on Educationally Disadvantaged Children of Pre-school Age'. Unpublished doctoral dissertation, Monash University, Victoria.

COSGROVE, J. M. and PATTERSON, S. J. (1977) 'Plans and the development of listener skills'. *Developmental Psychology*, **13**, 557–564.

FLAVELL, J. H. (1977) 'Metacognitive development'. Paper presented at NATO Advanced Study Institute on Structural/Process Theories of Complex Human Behaviour, Banff, Alberta, Canada.

FLAVELL, J. A., BOTKIN, P. T., FRY, C. L., WRIGHT, J. W. and JARVIS, P. E. (1968) *The Development of Role-Taking and Communication Skills in Children*. New York: Wiley.

FRY, C. L. (1966) 'Training children to communicate to listeners'. *Child Development*, **37**, 674–685.

FRY, C. L. (1969) 'Training children to communicate to listeners who have varying listener requirements'. *Journal of Genetic Psychology*, **114**, 153–166.

GLUCKSBERG, S., KRAUSS, R. and HIGGINS, E. T. (1975) 'The development of referential communication skills'. In HOROWITZ, F. D. (Ed.) *Review of Child Development Research*, **Vol. 4**. Chicago: University of Chicago Press.

HALLIDAY, M. A. K. (1975) *Learning How to Mean*. London: Arnold.

IRONSMITH, M. and WHITEHURST, G. J. (1978) 'The development of listener abilities in communication: how children deal with ambiguous information'. *Child Development*, **49**, 348–352.

LABOV, W. (1969) 'The logic of non-standard English'. In *Monograph Series on Language and Linguistics*, **22**, 1–31. Georgetown University, Washington, D.C.

MARATSOS, M. P. (1973) 'Nonegocentric communication abilities in preschool children'. *Child Development*, **44**, 697–700.

MARKMAN, E. M. (1977) 'Realizing that you don't understand: a preliminary investigation'. *Child Development*, **48**, 986–992.

MARKMAN, E. M. (1978) 'Comprehensive monitoring'. Paper presented at conference on Children's Oral Communication Skills, University of Wisconsin.

MENIG-PETERSON, C. L. (1975) 'The modification of the communicative behaviour in preschool-aged children as a function of the listener's perspective'. *Child Development*, **45**, 1015–1018.

PATTERSON, C. J., MASSAD, C. M. and COSGROVE, J. M. (1978) 'The Children's referential communication: components of plans for effective listening'. *Developmental Psychology*, **14**, 401–406.

PATTERSON, C. J. and KISTER, M. C. (1978) 'The development of listener skills for referential communication'. Paper presented at conference on Children's Oral Communication Skills, University of Wisconsin.

PIAGET, J. (1959) *The Language and Thought of the Child*. 3rd edition. London: Routledge and Kegan Paul. (First published 1926.)

PIAGET, J. (1962) 'Comments'. In VYGOTSKY, L. *Thought and Language*. Boston, Mass.: The M.I.T. Press.

ROBINSON, E. J. (1978) 'The child's understanding of inadequate messages and communication failure: a problem of ignorance or egocentrism?' Paper given at conference on Children's Oral Communication Skills, University of Wisconsin.

ROBINSON, E. J. and ROBINSON, W. P. (1976a) 'Development changes in the child's explanation of communication failure'. *Australian Journal of Psychology*, **28**, 155–165.

ROBINSON, E. J. and ROBINSON, W. P. (1976b) 'The young child's understanding of communication'. *Developmental Psychology*, **12**, 328–333.

ROBINSON, E. J. and ROBINSON, W. P. (1977a) 'Development in the understanding of causes of success and failure'. *Cognition*, **5**, 363–378.

ROBINSON, E. J. and ROBINSON, W. P. (1977b) 'The young child's explanations of communication failure: a re-interpretation of results'. *Perceptual and Motor Skills*, **44**, 363–366.

ROBINSON, E. J. and ROBINSON, W. P. (1978a) 'Explanations of communication failure and ability to give bad messages'. *British Journal of Social and Clinical Psychology*, **17**, 219–225.

ROBINSON, E. J. and ROBINSON, W. P. (1978b) 'Development of understanding about communication: message inadequacy and its role in causing communication failure'. *Genetic Psychological Monographs*, **98**, 233–279.

ROBINSON, E. J. and ROBINSON, W. P. (1978c) 'The roles of egocentrism and of weakness in comparing in children's explanations of communication failure'. *Journal of Experimental Child Psychology*, **26**, 147–160.

ROBINSON, E. J. and ROBINSON, W. P. (1979) 'Ways of reacting to communication failure in relation to the development of the child's understanding about verbal communication'. Manuscript submitted for publication.

ROSENBERG, S. and COHEN, B. D. (1966) 'Referential processes of speakers and listeners'. *Psychological Review*, **73**, 208–231.

RYLE, G. (1949) *The Concept of Mind*. Oxford: Oxford University Press.

SHANTZ, C. V. and WILSON, K. (1972) 'Training communication skills in young children'. *Child Development*, **43**, 118–122.

SHATZ, M. (1978) 'The relationship between cognitive processes and the development of communication skills'. In KEAREY (Ed.) *Nebraska Symposium on Motivation, 1977*. Lincoln: University of Nebraska Press.

SHATZ, M. and GELMAN, R. (1973) The development of communication skills: modification in the speech of young children as a function of listener. *Monographs of the Society for Research in Child Development*, Serial No. 152.

VYGOTSKY, L. (1962) *Thought and Language*. Cambridge, Mass.: The M.I.T. Press.

WHITEHURST, G. J. and SONNENSCHEIN, S. (1978a) 'The development of communication: attribute variation leads to contrast failure'. *Journal of Experimental Child Psychology*, **25**, 454–490.

WHITEHURST, G. J. and SONNENSCHEIN, S. (1978b) 'The development of informative messages in referential communication'. Paper presented at conference on Children's Oral Communication Skills, University of Wisconsin.

7

The social concomitants of role-taking

PAUL LIGHT

Introduction

Role-taking has been defined as 'the tendency to perceive and conceptualize the interaction between oneself and another as seen through the other's eyes' (Selman, 1970, p. 3). Taking the role of another thus involves putting oneself in the place of another person and making inferences concerning his capabilities, attributes, expectations, feelings, and potential reactions.

Although Selman stresses that role-taking is 'a prototypical social-cognitive skill' (p. 3), most researchers have treated it as a *cognitive* skill with only some, usually unspecified, social implications. The aim of this chapter is to provide a counterweight to this tendency by considering role-taking development in relation to social behaviour and social experience.

Since Piaget and Inhelder reported their 'three-mountains' study in 1956 the notion of childhood egocentrism (an absence of role-taking) has become largely identified with the problem of the coordination of *visual* perspectives. Similar kinds of tasks have been used by more recent researchers (e.g. Coie, Constanzo and Farnill, 1973; Pufall, 1975) to investigate the spatial and cognitive aspects of perspective-taking. Nigl and Fishbein (1974) went so far as to construct their task in such a way that the possibility of egocentric errors (in which the child selects his own view) was eliminated because, they argued, these errors would obscure the phenomenon under study, viz. the child's understanding of the projective relationships among objects.

It is clear (and was clear to Piaget), however, that more is involved in the inability to predict another's visual perspective than is usually connoted by the term 'egocentrism' (see chapter by Cox). Likewise there is more to egocentrism than the inability to construct visual perspectives. As Flavell (1968) pointed out, any prediction of the content of another's view depends upon the child's awareness of the existence of perspective differences and of the *need* to take account of them. The child's tendency to select his own view in a typical perspective-taking task may arise not from an inadequacy of visuo-spatial schemata but rather from a failure to recognize that the situation demands the employment of such schemata. If we say of an adult that he is 'being egocentric' we do not usually mean that he is cognitively deficient and incapable of the inferences involved in taking another's perspective. Rather, we mean that he does not feel the necessity to accommodate to the other's viewpoint, or that he is *insensitive* to it. One sense in which young children might be regarded as egocentric, then, is if they showed a generalized lack of sensitivity to alternative viewpoints.

A large number of the more 'cognitive' studies (reviewed by Shantz, 1975) suggest that the ability to coordinate visual perspectives is a function of the particular task presented, and that in some circumstances nonegocentric responses may be elicited at least as early as the second or third years of life. Other approaches to study of early role-taking have yielded similar results. Social guessing games have been used (Flavell, 1968 ; De Vries, 1970), as have communication tasks in which measures are obtained of the extent to which the child takes his listener's role attributes into account (Maratsos, 1973; Krauss and Glucksberg, 1977). Children's ability to handle privileged information has been studied (Flavell, 1968 ; Chandler, 1972). The affective side of role-taking has been investigated by Borke (1971, 1973). The general picture which emerges from these studies is that some basic forms of role-taking emerge very early in childhood but that they are initially fragile, situation specific, and heavily dependent upon contextual and instuctional cues.

A number of authors report a marked gap between availability of inferential skills and the use made of them (Levine and Hoffman, 1975; Acredolo, 1977), while Flavell remarks that: 'Whatever the underlying cause, the net effect is a marked gap between our hypothetical child's developed *capabilities* for social cognition and the amount of social cognition he *spontaneously* carries out' (1974, p. 76). Flavell uses the following example: a child of six years or more might quite typically say 'you put that thing in the cup' when explaining something to a listener who, being blindfolded or behind a screen, cannot see the object to which the child is referring. In interpreting this 'egocentric communication failure' it would presumably be wrong to suppose that the child actively believes that his listener *can* see, and presumably also wrong to presume that he considers his message to be adequate for a listener who *cannot* see. It seems rather that he fails to pay attention to his listener and thus fails to see the need to adapt his message to his listener's needs.

Individual differences and their generality

In Flavell's (1968) studies of role-taking he repeatedly observed a very wide range of individual differences between children of the same age. Other authors (e.g. Hughes, 1975) have made the same observations – where several age groups are studied the individual variation within one age group may be very large relative to the differences between age groups. Such individual differences raise a number of interesting questions, the first of which concerns their generality. There are, as we have observed, a wide range of possible approaches to the measurement of role-taking skills. If we can speak of role-taking as a general skill (or disposition) then individual differences should be reasonably stable across a range of tasks. Put simply, if we give a number of tasks all supposedly tapping role-taking skills to the same children, will the children who are good at one of them be good at all of them?

Rubin (1973) has examined patterns of performance of 5 to 11-year-olds across a range of tasks. He included a measure of egocentric or private speech, a measure of spatial egocentrism, a measure of recursiveness of thinking, and a measure of communicational accuracy. Analysis indicated a cluster of substantial intercorrelations between these tasks, with the exception of the private speech measures. A principal components analysis yielded further support in the form of a first factor accounting for over 50 % of the variance on which the role-taking tasks (excepting private speech) all loaded heavily. The results for private speech may be seen as supporting Vygotsky's (1962) interpretation of such speech as having a positive developmental function (cognitive self-guidance) rather than simply exemplifying egocentrism.

Hollos and Cowan (1973; Hollos, 1975) administered a version of the three-mountains task, Flavell's picture story task, and a communicational accuracy task to seven- to nine-year-old children in Norway and subsequently in Hungary. They also gave the same children a range of logical operations tasks. Their results seemed to give some confirmation of the statistical unitariness of the role-taking measures. A principal components analysis of all the scores suggested two interpretable components, one which was strongly associated with the role-taking tasks. The communicational accuracy task was the only one of the 'role-taking group' which loaded heavily on the factor associated with logical operations.

A study by Van Lieshout, Leckie and Smits-Van Sonsbeck (1973) also found significant intercorrelations between eight out of nine role-taking tasks administered to three- to five-year-olds, with one major factor on which all eight tasks loaded emerging from the factor analysis.

Not all studies have suggested a unitary role-taking factor. Urberg and Docherty (1976) gave five affective role-taking tasks to three- to six-year-olds and identified two clusters: the three tasks requiring sequential perspective-taking forming one group and the two requiring simultaneous coordination of perspectives forming another. A number of other studies have found evidence of multiple factors or complex age- and sex-dependent relationships (Kurdek and Rodgon, 1975; Kurdek, 1977; O'Connor, 1977).

The review by Shantz (1975) includes a number of unpublished studies which bear on this question. Some have quite failed to find significant intercorrelations, although Shantz points out that low correlations might be artefacts due to poor reliability, limitations of scoring, or variable difficulty levels. She concludes that while some studies have shown 'unexpectedly high' levels of correlation, the overall picture is of only moderate relationships amongst various role-taking skills.

The origin of individual differences

Theoretical starting points for an examination of causal interdependences between social and nonsocial aspects of cognition may be found in the work of Piaget (e.g. 1950) and in that of G. H. Mead (1934). Mead argued strongly that social experience had a determining effect upon general cognitive development and that this effect was mediated by social role-taking. It should, therefore, be possible to show systematic relationships between the development of role-taking and the quality of experienced social interactions. Piaget's position is more equivocal: role-taking is seen both as reflecting, and as being reflected in, other aspects of cognitive development. But in eschewing simple causal models Piaget is not denying that role-taking is potentially susceptible to the influence of specific kinds of social experience.

In the discussion of how egocentrism is overcome, Piaget (1928, 1950) has placed primary emphasis upon the child's interactions with his peers. He argues that the social relation of reciprocity, which he sees as crucial, arises between individuals considering themselves as equals. Flavell (1968) suggests that the influence of peer group participation may be better conceptualized as providing general role-taking opportunities than having very specific or unique forms of influence. He emphasizes the possible importance of interactions with certain non-peers, including adults and younger children. He suggests, for instance, that the child who has a somewhat younger sibling may well have particularly good opportunities to stretch his role-taking capabilities. Kohlberg (1969), discussing moral judgement as a special aspect of the development of role-taking, further plays down the importance of the peer group, concluding that the limited evidence available does not support the idea that participation in the peer group plays any critical or unique role in moral development.

Hollos and Cowan's studies in Norway and Hungary were mentioned in the previous section. They studied logical operations and role-taking abilities in children living in town, in small villages, and in isolated farms. Opportunity for peer interaction decreased from the towns to the farms. They found little effect of social setting upon logical operations (if anything the isolated farm children were superior) and age effects were prominent. But with role-taking the social setting effects predominated, the socially isolated farm children performing very poorly compared to town and village children. However, there was no difference between the latter groups despite the town children having more experience of social interaction. Hollos and Cowan suggest a 'threshold model', in which a minimum of social interaction is a necessary prerequisite of role-taking development, but beyond this level more opportunity for interaction has little effect. Nahir and Yussen (1977) have shown differences favouring Israeli Kibbutz children compared to city children on measures of communicative role-taking, which they interpret in terms of the higher level of peer interactions in the Kibbutz. West (1974), however, finding no differences in role-taking between Kibbutz and city children, interpreted this as meaning that both groups were 'above threshold' in Hollos and Cowan's sense.

Both Flavell and Kohlberg suggest that participation in social interaction in the home probably provides the major setting for role-taking opportunities, but they give little guidance as to the types of home which might foster role-taking ability. The finding that 'inductive' styles of parental discipline are associated with advanced moral development in the child (Hoffman, 1970) is perhaps relevant, given the association between moral judgement and role-taking (e.g. Ambron and Irwin, 1975). 'Inductive' control involves the giving of reasons and the pointing out of consequences. Shantz (1975) remarks that the parent's verbal explicitness about his own and other people's responses to the child's behaviour bears an almost 'face valid' relationship to the development of the child's role-taking ability. At the other extreme, punishment-oriented discipline is associated with poor moral development, and Piaget has himself suggested that social systems based on authority may hinder the process of decentration (Piaget, 1970).

Basil Bernstein's distinction between 'personal' and 'positional' modes of relation within the family seems to provide a means of clarifying the issues involved here. Bernstein (1970) hs argued for a close relationship between linguistic codes, role-taking, and the prevailing character of the role relationships: 'An elaborated code encourages the speaker to focus upon the experience of others, as different from his own. In the case of a restricted code, what is transmitted verbally usually refers to the other person in terms of common group or status membership. Thus restricted codes could be considered status or positional codes whereas elaborated codes are oriented to persons' (p. 476). Bernstein, acknowledging his idebtedness to Mead, sees the origins of different linguistic codes in the role structure of the family, influencing the child particularly through the means of social control employed. He suggests that in a 'person-oriented' family the child's developing self is differentiated by continuous adjustment to the verbally realized intentions and motives of others. In the positional family the child responds to status requirements, learning a communalized as opposed to an individualised role.

Bernstein and Cook (1968) developed a coding frame dealing with distinctions between various forms of verbal control, utilized subsequently by Brandis and Henderson (1970) and Cook-Gumperz (1973). Some evidence of the relationship between such measures of family interaction and the child's role-taking abilities has been provided by Bearison and Cassel (1975). Children from predominantly person-oriented families showed greater evidence of accommodating their communication to a blindfolded as opposed to a sighted listener than children from predominantly position-oriented families.

Before leaving the question of role-taking opportunities we should note that these may not always take the form of actual social exchanges. It may be that the overt or covert playing out of roles in solitary play is also significant (Mead, 1934). The child may not only practise adult roles, but also role-taking activities like those involved in competitive or cooperative situations. He may rehearse past or future interactions with others, imagining the responses of another occupying a complementary role. In these respects solitary play may provide an important context for role-taking development.

Role-taking and social behaviour

The ability to take the role of another is basic to the ability to comprehend and predict the other's behaviour, so that role-taking can be seen as a prerequisite for many types of social behaviour (Hartup, 1970). This being so, it is natural to consider how individual differences in role-taking are related to individual differences in social behaviour. Available evidence is confusing and conflicting, perhaps partly because few of the studies have used a sufficiently wide variety either of role-taking tasks or of indices of social behaviour.

Zahn-Waxler, Radke-Yarrow and Brady-Smith (1977) did use a battery of role-taking measures but did not find scores to be predictive of 'prosocial interventions' (comforting, helping and sharing) made by three- to seven-year-olds. Jennings (1975) likewise failed to show a relationship between role-taking and observational measures of preference for interaction with people as opposed to objects. However, Jennings' role-taking measures did show positive relationships with ratings of popularity, peer leadership, and other aspects of social competence. Rothenberg (1970) found an affective role-taking measure to be positively related to peer and teacher ratings of leadership, gregariousness and friendship in eight- to ten-year-olds. As to cooperation, Levine and Hoffman (1975) were unable to show a relationship between affective role-taking and cooperative behaviour in four-year-olds, though they point to some evidence of such a relationship at later ages. Johnson (1975) did find significant relationships between affective role-taking and cooperation in 11-year-olds.

Available evidence on the relationship of role-taking abilities and social adjustment in normal children is thus fairly equivocal. The same can be said of attempts to show effects on cooperative or altruistic behaviour by training normal children in social role-taking skills. Some success has been claimed (e.g. Staub, 1971) but other large-scale and careful studies such as that of Wentink and colleagues (1975) in Holland have failed to show any substantial effects. The evidence from studies of seriously maladjusted children is perhaps more convincing. Neale, in 1966, found that emotionally disturbed, aggressive children tended to show very poor role-taking skills. Chandler (1972, 1973) has extended this line of enquiry, using chronically delinquent and emotionally disturbed boys. Using a picture story technique he found that, with some exceptions, the disturbed or delinquent children were markedly deficient in role-taking. The typical disturbed child of 13 remained more egocentric than seven-year-olds in a control group matched for socioeconomic and ethnic background. Chandler ran an 'actors workshop' for a group of delinquent children, making extensive use of videotape etc., and claimed to show a significant improvement in role-taking abilities even when compared with another group who were involved in the making of documentary films. Eighteen-month follow-ups showed significant reductions in known delinquent behaviour, though Chandler observes that their improved social skills may be reflected in being better able to avoid being caught! Chandler, Greenspan and Barenboim (1974) have also carried out a 12-month follow-up of the effects of training institutionalized emotionally disturbed children in role-taking and communication skills, and found evidence of improvements in social adjustment.

To summarize, then, there is limited and somewhat conflicting evidence as to the existence of a positive relationship between role-taking and social competence in normal young children. There seems to be rather better evidence, at least for older children, of a negative relationship between role-taking and seriously disturbed or antisocial behaviour.

A research project

Flavell has commented that 'it can now be taken as fact that ... the developmental *rate* of skill acquisition in this area is enormously variable from child to child' (1968, p. 218). He went on to add that 'we should like to know just what qualities of characteristics of the individual and of his environment during the formative years contribute to or impede the attainment of these skills' (p. 220). The remainder of this chapter will be devoted to an account of a research project which addressed this question. It was designed to clarify the issue of the generality of individual differences in role-taking, and to study the concomitants of such differences in the domains of social experience and social behaviour.

The research was conducted by the author as part of a longitudinal study of mothers and children in Cambridge, England, directed by Martin Richards. Details of initial sample selection can be found in Richards and Bernal (1972). Present data are based upon approximately 60 mother–child pairs, reasonably representative in social class terms, all the children being first or second born.

The role-taking measures

Within a week or so after their fourth birthday the children were visited at home and given a variety of tasks designed as indices of role-taking. All the tasks were piloted to establish their appropriateness for this age group. All gave a wide spread of results, with some of the four-year-olds performing errorlessly and some completely 'egocentrically'. The tasks themselves and the absolute levels of performance will only be described briefly here, since our present concern is chiefly with individual differences and their concomitants. Full details can be found in Light (1979).

The initial tasks concentrated on perspective taking in a literal, visual sense. The first two, termed Orientation tasks, involved the child's recognition that when a picture lies on a table between two people, if it is the right-way-up for one of them, it is upside-down for the other. The first task, modified from Flavell (1968), employed a simplified, two-dimensional human figure. The child was given a series of instructions to orient the figure so that he himself could see it the right-way-up (or upside-down), or so that the observer, sitting opposite, could see it up the right way (or upside-down). Some 20 % of the children followed these instuctions without error, while over 25 % always oriented the figure with respect to themselves regardless of instructions, the remainder being intermediate between these extremes. In the second task the observer and child again sat opposite one another, each having a set of cards. Each card bore a single picture. The observer, beginning the game, 'chose a present' for the child from his pictures and placed it with the child's cards, rotating it so as to be the right-way-up for the child. Roles of giver and receiver were alternated, the measure being of whether the child respected the observer's viewpoint in making presentations to him. Nearly 20 % of the children did so on all occasions, behaving as if the rotation of the pictures into the other's perspective was an obvious and 'natural' response. At the other extreme over 30 % of the children, with equal assuredness, oriented all cards with respect to themselves.

The next two tasks, termed Interposition tasks, involved the child's recognition that when an object is interposed between two people, then if one person can see a particular side of the object, the other can only see the opposite side. The object employed was a regular tetrahedron with pictures pasted to three of its faces. When standing on a table it formed a three-sided pyramid such that if the observer was looking directly at one of its faces, the child could see the other two, and *vice versa*. In the first interposition task, after familiarization with the pictures, the child hid his eyes while the observer rotated the pyramid to look directly at one of its faces. The child was then allowed to look, and asked to work out what the observer was looking at. Roles were exchanged over a series of trials. In the second interposition game the pyramid remained in a fixed position and a doll was placed at various points in relation to it, the child having to say on each trial which face or faces of the pyramid the doll could see. For both tasks a good spread of scores was obtained.

The next two tasks, termed Hiding tasks, were essentially versions of 'hide and seek' played with dolls. The child had to place a doll so that it could not be seen by one (or more than one) other doll. He had thus to recognize that where objects were interposed between searcher and sought, then the searcher's view would be obstructed. In the first hiding game the child had to hide one doll from another amongst a group of 'obstacles' arranged for the purpose. The initial position of the searcher doll varied over four trials, so that a position which was a good hiding place on one occasion might not be on the next. Only 10 % of the children hid the doll successfully on all trials. The second hiding task involved one doll being hidden from two others. The obstacles used were rather simpler than those used in the first task and were arranged so that with the two searchers placed orthogonally to the array, only one position constituted a satisfactory hiding place for the third doll on each trial. Some 20 % of the children hid the doll correctly on all four trials, while nearly 30 % made several uncorrected errors.

The next task was termed Penny-hiding, and was modelled on De Vries' (1970) study. The observer showed the child a penny, hid it in one of his hands behind his back and, bringing out two fisted hands, asked the child to guess which hand the penny was in. After a number of guessing trials the child was asked to hide the penny, and scoring was based upon the child's competence in managing the concealment. Most of the children seemed to be able to deal with the notion that they could open their hands and swap the penny about while it was behind their back but not while it was in front of them. The majority, however, were not able regularly to bring out their fisted hands and hold them symmetrically. They would often bring out only one hand, or hold one of them open. Thus it was not usually difficult for the observer to tell which hand the penny was in, quite apart from the give-away predictability of sequence which was characteristic of so many of the children.

The final task (Faces) was modelled on studies by Borke (1971, 1973). The children were told a series of short stories relating to a character who was represented by a figure devoid of a face. A set of alternative faces was available; each face had a different emotional expression. After each story the child had to place the appropriate face on the figure, according to how he though that figure would be feeling. A somewhat complex scoring system was necessitated by the response biases shown, but only 5 % of the children responded correctly on all nine trials.

We have thus a motley assortment of tasks, all fairly contrived and artificial. To answer the question of the generality of the role-taking concept we must examine the intercorrelations of scores. If performance is determined to a substantial degree by a general sensitivity to others' perceptives, then, despite their dissimilarities, all the tasks should be substantially intercorrelated.

Interrelationships between tasks

Details of the derivation of scores from each of the tasks, and details of the analysis

TABLE 1 Intercorrelations of role-taking scores (*p<0.05, 2 tailed)

	1	2	3	4	5	6	7	8
1 (Orientation 1)	+0.52*	+0.42*	+0.34*	+0.24	+0.35*	+0.37*	+0.45*
2 (Orientation 2)		+0.38*	+0.32*	+0.37*	+0.45*	+0.48*	+0.46*
3 (Interposition 0)			+0.40*	+0.33*	+0.12	+0.45*	+0.56*
4 (Interposition-Doll)				+0.19	+0.24	+0.54*	+0.33*
5 (Hiding A)					+0.59*	+0.43*	+0.46*
6 (Hiding B)						+0.40*	+0.32*
7 (Penny Hiding)							+0.51*
8 (Faces)							

summarized here, may be found in Light (1979). Intercorrelations of the eight scores are shown in Table 1. Of the 28 coefficients, 24 are statistically significant, and the overall picture is of a uniform and quite substantial degree of correlation. A Principal Components Analysis showed a very large first component, upon which all eight tasks loaded about equally, and which accounted for approximately 50 % of the total variance.

To establish the extent to which the correlations in Table 1 arose from a 'general intelligence' factor, Stanford Binet IQ Scores were obtained for each child and the correlation matrix recalculated with IQ variance partialled out. All the partial correlations were still positive and 21 of the 28 still statistically significant. So while it is true that the role-taking measures were positively correlated with IQ, this was not sufficient to account for their homogenity. Some children were very much better than others on all role-taking tasks, and this was not simply as a function of higher IQ.

In order to examine the concomitants of being a 'good role-taker', a single score was derived from each child by using a simple total from the eight tasks. The means and standard deviations of scores were sufficiently similar for this to be justified. The resulting score, presumptively termed a role-taking score, will be examined in relation to other material available from the study of the children at four years of age, and also from earlier and later ages, to sketch some possible antecedents and consequences of being a good or a poor role-taker.

Role-taking and social adjustment

As noted earlier in this chapter, a number of authors (e.g. Piaget and Inhelder, 1969) have suggested that cooperative behaviour and effective communication depend upon role-taking, while other studies (e.g. Chandler, 1972, 1973) suggest a link between delinquent behaviour and failure of role-taking amongst adolescents. Within the 'normal' population of this study, is there evidence of a sytematic link between role-taking performance and social adjustment?

One way to answer this question is in terms of whether the four-year-olds' role-taking scores are predictive of maladjustment a year and a half later when the children are in their first year at school. Bristol Social Adjustment Guides were completed by the teachers at this stage. Six children scored as appreciably maladjusted in an *under-reactive* sense (Stott, 1971), and these six were indeed significantly poorer scorers on the role-taking measure than the remainder (though not of significantly lower IQ). Only one child scores as appreciably maladjusted in an over-reactive sense, this being the child who had scored least well on role-taking at four years of age. So from a small extreme group within the sample there is some evidence of an association between poor performance on the role-taking tasks and poor social adjustment.

Earlier, when the children were three years of age, an interview with the mother probed a variety of aspects of the child's social behaviour, and mothers were also asked to sort cards according to whether the statement each card bore seemed to describe their child or not. Children who at four were adept role-takers were more frequently classified at three as being friendly to strangers, willing to be left in the care of others and eager to explore novel surroundings. They tended at three to be better able to amuse themselves and to be less frequently bored than the poor role-takers. All of these relationships were statistically significant, while none of these aspects of social behaviour at three were related to IQ a year later. Some rather less predictable relationships also emerged: the adept role-takers were described as significantly more prone to whining, fussing and shouting to get their own way, and more prone to temper tantrums and bouts of bad behaviour. Incidentally they also seemed to be more prone to occasional wetting and soiling 'accidents'. While any interpretation of these relationships must be speculative, perhaps these findings should remind us that we have no good grounds for expecting the concomitants of adept role-taking to be invariably socially desirable. Teasing and lying are examples of negatively regarded behaviours which demand social role-taking. In adult life an obvious example is the 'confidence trickster' who relies for his success on his ability to predict and manipulate deceitfully the beliefs of others.

So in general terms we may say of the children who score well on social role-taking at four years that they are more socially confident and socially independent at three and that they are less likely to show appreciable maladjustment later when they go to school. On the other hand the interview material raises considerable doubts as the whether they are necessarily more amenable or easier to manage. Role-taking, it seems, is no panacea.

Role-taking and the mother–child relationship

The role-taking score showed no significant social class differences, using the Registrar General's Index of father's occupations, and also no significant sex differences. However, there was a parity difference. All the children in the sample were first-born or second-born, almost all the first-borns having younger siblings by the time they reached four years of age. Second borns had significantly better role-taking scores than first borns. There was no parity difference in IQ scores. This observation might seem to fit with the emphasis which Piaget puts upon child–child interaction in the overcoming of egocentrism. However, data from interviews with the mothers and diaries kept by them did not suggest any simple relationship between amount of contact with other children and the role-taking score. The diary material did show a relationship in rather crude terms between the role-taking score and the amount of adult attention. It, therefore, seemed worthwhile to examine qualitative aspects of mother–child interaction patterns to see whether they showed systematic relationships with the child's role-taking.

Detailed observational measures of 'attachment' between mother and baby in the first year were available. These covered measures such as mother smiling or looking at the baby, touching, caressing, responsiveness to crying, etc. These attachment indices were interrelated in rather complex ways (see Dunn, 1975) and showed a complete absence of significant relationships with the four-year-olds' role-taking measure.

However, contemporary measures of a rather different kind at four years did suggest a close relationship between role-taking and qualitative aspects of the mother–child relationship. Rather detailed information was available from a maternal interview on questions of discipline and social control. These data were analyzed in terms of Bernstein's (1970) distinction between *personal* and *positional* modes of relation, introduced earlier in this chapter. By a personal relation, Bernstein means one which is based upon perception of the individual attributes of the other, whereas a positional relation is based upon the status attributes of the other. Bernstein and Cook (1968; Cook-Gumpertz, 1973) have developed a detailed system for categorizing mothers' accounts of social control and discipline along these lines.

In the present study the mothers' rationales and strategies of social control were examined in this light. Personal rationales were those which justified a mother's action in terms of her perception of the motives or temperamental characteristics of the child, or to herself. For example: 'If she's really ashamed of herself, then ...' or 'She gets me in such a temper that ...' The frequency of such rationales was significantly associated with the child's role-taking score.

As to actual strategies, a number are identified by Bernstein and Cook as embodying aspects of a 'personal' relationship:

Avoidance (of interference), e.g. of the siblings quarrelling: 'usually if I can stand it it wears itself out'.

Emotional Support, e.g. of temper tantrums: 'feeling embarrassed is often the cause, I'll have to really cuddle him and comfort him'.

Concessions, e.g. when the child declines to come on mother's request: 'well if it's not too vital and she thinks she's busy I let her get on with it'.

As predicted each of these strategies was significantly more commonly mentioned by the mothers of 'good role takers'. In contrast, frequency of *physical punishment* (dependent upon positional relations of authority) was significantly negatively correlated with the role-taking score.

Of these relationships, only the punishment and concessions categories were significantly associated with IQ, and rather surprisingly none was associated significantly with social class. Granting the limitations of the present sample for examining social class differences, it is worth noting that in Cook-Gumpertz's (1973) larger London sample there was an absence of marked social class differences in many of the personal dimensions of social control.

Impressionistically, the most striking difference between families in terms of the role-taking score was in the degree of *symmetry* of the mother–child relationship. As an example, the mother of the lowest scoring child on role-taking gave the following answer to a question as to what she did when the child declined to do something for her because he was occupied in play: 'I usually say: "You'll do it now, I've told you to do it". I don't like the way some people perhaps say "Will you do this for me?" and then don't insist.' As a contrast, the mother of the child in the highest score on role-taking answered: 'Yes, she'll perhaps not do it straight away, but then I'm like that. If I'm busy doing something I'll say "well wait a minute", so it works both ways I suppose.'

These two quotations bring out the contrast between the non-reversible relationship of authority and the symmetrical relationship of negotiated equality. Piaget has suggested that: 'the social relation of reciprocity gradually imposes itself as a form of equilibrium between individuals considering themselves as equals' (1960, p. 20). Piaget saw the requisite equality in the peer relationship. Present findings would suggest that, despite the obvious inequalities of the mother–child relationship, the capacity of the mother to consider the child *as if he were* an equal may play a critical part in developing the child's social sensitivity.

Discussion and conclusions

Piaget and Inhelder's (1956) studies of visual perspective-taking seemed to show that children were not able to make accurate, nonegocentric predictions concerning another's point of view until at least seven or eight years of age. Many of the more recent studies, however, clearly point to the conclusion that preschool children are not profoundly egocentric. Children as young as two or three years of age can manage certain very basic inferences about other people's viewpoints. As Shantz (1975) concludes from her review of this work, the preschooler has emerged as much more competent in his social understanding than we have given him credit for being. The results from the role-taking tasks employed in the present study certainly demonstrate that four-year-olds are by no means totally egocentric.

Research in this area has often been directed at the specification of 'ages and stages' in the development of role-taking ability (e.g. Selman, 1973; Flavell, 1974). However, a good deal of difficulty has been encountered in the attempts to apply simple models of successive stages. Tasks supposedly tapping the same levels of role-taking may produce widely differing performances, and apparently minor details of task design or of response requirement often seem to make a great deal of difference to the difficulty of the task (e.g. Weinheimer, 1972; Eiser, 1977). There is a tendency to assume that differences in group performance between different tasks must directly affect the presence or absence of competence for a particular level of role-taking inference. But a number of authors (e.g. Flavell, 1974; Levine and Hoffman, 1975) have suggested that there may in fact be a considerable gap between the availability of the inferential skills involved and the spontaneous *use* of such skills in any given situation. Acredolo's (1977) observation that prompting is very effective in improving the spatial perspective-taking performance of four-year-olds is consistent with this view. Indeed, if we accept the evidence of such recent studies as Masangkay, McCluskey, McIntyre, Sims-Knight, Vaughn and Flavell (1974) or Lempers, Flavell and Flavell (1977) we might reasonably conclude that all of the children tested in the present study should have had the requisite competences to succeed in most if not all of the tasks. They manifestly did not do so, and it is with the individual differences in success and failure that we have here been mainly concerned. If a distinction is made between competence and performance, then, our emphasis is on the latter.

Individual differences may, we suggest, be largely governed by the degree of sensitivity shown by the child to the role-taking requirements of the situation. The adoption of this emphasis on the sensitivity of the child to perspective differences and of the need to adapt to them brings us much closer to role-taking differences as we understand them amongst adults. As noted earlier, a certain piece of adult behaviour may be construed as egocentric (i.e. as reflecting a failure to see another's point of view) without it being implied that the adult concerned lacks knowledge of the existence of perspective differences or is incapable of taking account of them. In children, just as in adults, it may be appropriate for some purposes to treat role-taking as a disposition, or 'habit of thinking', rather than as a series of quasi-logical acquisitions. This approach naturally undermines attempts at structural analysis in terms of developmental stages. Indeed it suggests that the same kinds of things which govern individual differences in adulthood *may* also govern comparable individual differences amongst young children.

Using a total score derived from the eight role-taking tasks, characteristics of the children and their families were investigated in order to discover some of the concomitants of the marked individual differences in role-taking. To some extent IQ was used as a crude 'control' measure, interest centering on those relationships with the role-taking measure which are not accountable for by reference to shared dependence on 'general intelligence'.

Very little is known about how role-taking, in the sense in which we have used the term, is related to everyday social interaction. Even if one accepts that social interaction must be heavily dependent upon social role-taking, one is not bound to accept that the ongoing flow of largely unconsidered social adjustments can be indexed by a series of role-taking tasks such as those used here. Moreover it is by no means clear what aspects of social behaviour we should expect to be associated with adept role-taking. The lack of clear cut evidence on the ways in which specific types of social interaction influence children's social understanding, and *vice versa*, was noted earlier in this chapter.

Evidence on this question obtained from the present study was indirect, being based upon the reports of mothers and teachers. The children who at age four years were good role-takers apparently had shown the following characteristics at three years: they were more friendly towards strangers, more willing to be left in the care of others, and more confident in novel surroundings; they were less heavily dependent upon the mother's presence to support their activities and were rarely bored. However, at age three good role-taking also seemed to be associated with frequent temper and bad behaviour and with the child fussing to get his own way. It is interesting to note that Kurdek (1978) has also found a number of troublesome behaviours to be associated with good role-taking.

The analysis of the Bristol Social Adjustment Guide material, obtained from the schools when the children were aged $5\frac{1}{2}$ years, lent some support to the association of poor role-taking with maladjustment. The relatively small numbers of children obtaining substantial maladjustment scores had been significantly poorer role-takers than the remainder at four years.

With certain interesting exceptions at three years, then, these relationships are consistent with sensitive role-takers being socially confident and accommodating easily to new relationships and new social situations such as the school.

The present study also examined the relationship between the role-taking sensitivity of the child and the quality of the mother–child relationship. As noted earlier, Flavell, Kohlberg and others have suggested that the pattern of social interaction in the child's family may be crucial for role-taking development, but the literature offers little empirical evidence on this question.

Again we have relied on interview material, and the kinds of things the mothers said about their children, or about their own behaviour, may not have corresponded directly with what actually went on in the family. Nevertheless a consistent pattern of relationships emerged between how the mothes answered the questions and how well the children performed on the role-taking tasks. The prediction that a high degree of role-taking sensitivity should be related to a highly 'personal' maternal style was clearly supported.

The personal-positional dichotomy can be conceptualized in terms of whether the mother acted towards, or spoke of, the child *as a person*. The 'symmetry' noted in relation to some of the answers to interview questions did not imply that the child was treated as an adult rather than as a child. It implied that he was treated as an autonomous individual, possessed of his own thoughts and feelings, his own likes and dislikes and so on. In this sense, of course, one may see such personal control as an indication of the role-taking sensitivity of the mother.

The restriction of attention to the mother represents an obvious limitation. Whether the mother's role is crucial or whether the mother's behaviour and attitudes are simply a good guide to those of others with whom the child has contact remains an open question. Also left open is the question of the determinants of the mother's attitudes and behaviour. We cannot ignore the role of the child himself in the establishment of the mother's attitudes towards him. This interaction must have the form of a negotiation, and individual characteristics of the child must contribute to 'the sort of child his mother sees him as being'. The frequency with which the mothers in this study commented upon differences in the characters of their several children seemed to confirm this. However, it is just this kind of individuality to which highly 'person-oriented' mothers will be sensitive, so that they will treat their children very differently according to how they see their emotional needs. We have, then, to differentiate between a mother's disposition to be responsive to her children 'as persons' on the one hand, and the particular way she comes to see a given child on the other. The interactive basis of the latter is clear, while the former may well reflect a fairly stable aspect of the mother's personality.

Early in this chapter the theoretical writings of G. H. Mead were mentioned, with particular reference to the proposition that social experience had a determining effect upon general cognitive development and that this effect was mediated by social role-taking. Present results, insofar as they give support to the view that observed differences in role-taking are due in some part to different kinds of social experience within the family, provide support for one aspect of Mead's proposition. To this extent also, they seem to contradict the alternative argument that role-taking is simply a manifestation in the social sphere of general processes of individual cognitive development.

There is a real need for more detailed and delicate study of the relationship between cognitive development and experience in a social environment. Role-taking, as a concept which bridges social and individual aspects of cognition, seems to hold much promise for such an undertaking.

References

ACREDOLO, L. (1977) 'Developmental changes in the ability to coordinate perspectives of a large scale space'. *Developmental Psychology*, **13**, 1–8.

AMBRON, S. and IRWIN, D. (1975) 'Role-taking and moral judgement in five- and seven-year-olds'. *Developmental Psychology*, **11**, 102.

BEARISON, D. and CASSEL, T. (1975) 'Cognitive decentration and social codes: communicative effectiveness in young children from differing family contexts'. *Developmental Psychology*, **11**, 29–36.

BERNSTEIN, B. (1970) 'A sociolinguistic approach to socialization, with some reference to educability'. In GUMPERZ, J. and HYMES, D. (Eds.) *Directions in Sociolinguistics*. New York: Holt, Rinehart and Winston.

BERNSTEIN, B. and COOK, J. (1968) 'Coding grid for maternal control'. Available from Department of Sociology, University of London, Institute of Education.

BORKE, H. (1971) 'Interpersonal perception of young children: egocentrism or empathy?' *Developmental Psychology*, **5**, 263–269.

BORKE, H. (1973) 'The development of empathy in Chinese and American children between 3 and 6 years of age'. *Developmental Psychology*, **9**, 102–108.

BRANDIS, W. and HENDERSON, D. (1970) *Social Class, Language and Communication*. London: Routledge and Kegan Paul.

CHANDLER, M. (1972) 'Egocentrism in normal and pathological child development'. In MONKS, F., HARTUP, W. and DE WIT, J. (Eds.) *Determinants of Behavioural Development*. London: Academic Press.

CHANDLER, M. (1973) 'Egocentrism and antisocial behaviour: the assessment and training of social perspective-taking skills'. *Developmental Psychology*, **9**, 326–332.

CHANDLER, M., GREENSPAN, S. and BARENBOIM, C. (1974) 'Assessment and training of role-taking and referential communication skills in institutionalised emotionally disturbed children'. *Developmental Psychology*, **10**, 546–553.

COIE, J., COSTANZO, P. and FARNILL, D. (1973) 'Specific transitions in the development of spatial perspective-taking ability'. *Developmental Psychology*, **9**, 167–177.

COOK-GUMPERZ, J. (1973) *Social Control and Socialisation*. London: Routledge and Kegan Paul.

DE VRIES, R. (1970) 'The development of role-taking as reflected by the behaviour of bright, average and retarded children in a social guessing game'. *Child Development*, **41**, 759–770.

DUNN, J. (1975) 'Consistency and change in styles of mothering'. In *Parent–Infant Interaction*. Ciba Foundation symposium, **33** (new series), Amsterdam: Elsevier.

EISER, C. (1977) 'Strategies children use to coordinate perspectives as a function of task demands'. *British Journal of Educational Psychology*, **47**, 327–329.

FLAVELL, J. (1968) in collaboration with BOTKIN, P., FRY, C., WRIGHT, J. and JARVIS, P. *The Development of Role-Taking and Communication Skills in Children*. New York: Wiley.

FLAVELL, J. (1974) 'The development of inferences about others'. In MISCHEL, T. (Ed.) *Understanding Other Persons*. Oxford: Blackwell.

HARTUP, W. (1970) 'Peer interaction and social organisation'. In MUSSEN, P. (Ed.) *Carmichael's Manual of Child Psychology*. **Vol. 2.** New York: Wiley.

HOFFMAN, M. (1970) 'Moral development'. In MUSSEN, P. (Ed.) *Carmichael's Manual of Child Psychology*. **Vol. 2.** New York: Wiley.

HOLLOS, M. (1975) 'Logical operations and role-taking abilities in two cultures: Norway and Hungary'. *Child Development*, **46**, 638–649.

HOLLOS, M. and COWAN, P. (1973) 'Social isolation and cognitive development: logical operations and role-taking abilities in three Norwegian social settings'. *Child Development*, **44**, 630–641.

HUGHES, M. (1975) 'Egocentrism in Preschool Children'. Unpublished Ph.D. thesis, University of Edinburgh.

JENNINGS, K. (1975) 'People versus object orientation, social behaviour and intellectual abilities in preschool children'. *Developmental Psychology*, **11**, 511.

JOHNSON, D. (1975) 'Affective perspective-taking and co-operative predisposition'. *Developmental Psychology*, **11**, 869–870.

KOHLBERG, L. (1969) 'Stage and sequence: the cognitive-developmental approach to socialisation'. In GOSLIN, D. (Ed.) *Handbook of Socialisation: Theory and Research*. New York: Rand McNally.

KRAUSS, R. and GLUCKSBERG, S. (1977) 'Social and non-social speech'. *Scientific American*, **236**, 100–106.

KURDEK, L. (1977) 'Structural components and intellectual correlates of cognitive perspective taking in first through fourth grade children'. *Child Development*, **48**, 1503–1511.

KURDEK, L. (1978) 'Relationship between cognitive perspective taking and teachers' ratings of children's classroom behaviour in grades one through four'. *Journal of Genetic Psychology*, **132**, 21–28.

KURDEK, L. and RODGON, M. (1975) 'Perceptual, cognitive and affective perspective taking in kindergarten through sixth grade children'. *Developmental Psychology*, **11**, 643–650.

LEMPERS, J., FLAVELL, E. and FLAVELL, J. (1977) 'The development in very young children of tacit knowledge concerning visual perception'. *Genetic Psychology Monographs*, **95**, 3–53.

LEVINE, L. and HOFFMAN, M. (1975) 'Empathy and cooperation in four year olds'. *Developmental Psychology*, **11**, 533–534.

LIGHT, P. (1979) *The Growth of Social Sensitivity*. Cambridge: Cambridge University Press.

MARATSOS, M. (1973) 'Nonegocentric communication abilities in preschool children'. *Child Development*, **44**, 697–700.

MASANGKAY, Z., MCCLUSKEY, M., MCINTYRE, C., SIMS-KNIGHT, J., VAUGHN, B. and FLAVELL, J. (1974) 'The early development of inferences about the visual percepts of others'. *Child Development*, **45**, 357–366.

MEAD, G. H. (1934) In MORRIS, C. W. (Ed.) *Mind, Self and Society*. Chicago: University of Chicago Press.

NAHIR, H. and YUSSEN, S. (1977) 'The performance of Kibbutz and city reared Israeli children on two role-taking tasks'. *Developmental Psychology*, **13**, 450–455.

NEALE, J. (1966) 'Egocentrism in institutionalised and non-institutionalised children'. *Child Development*, **37**, 97–101.

NIGL, A. and FISHBEIN, H. (1974) 'Perception and conception in coordination of perspectives'. *Developmental Psychology*, **10**, 856–866.

O'CONNOR, M. (1977) 'The relationship of spatial and conceptual role-taking in children'. *Journal of Genetic Psychology*, **131**, 319–321.

PIAGET, J. (1928) *Judgement and Reasoning in the Child*. New York: Harcourt and Brace.

PIAGET, J. (1932) *The Moral Judgement of the Child*. London: Routledge and Kegan Paul.

PIAGET, J. (1950) *The Psychology of Intelligence*. London: Routledge and Kegan Paul.

PIAGET, J. (1960) 'The general problems of the psychobiological development of the child'. In TANNER, J. and INHELDER, B. (Eds.) *Discussions on Child Development*. **Vol. 4.** London: Tavistock.

PIAGET, J. (1970) 'Piaget's theory'. In MUSSEN, P. (Ed.) *Carmichael's Manual of Child Psychology*. **Vol. 1.** New York: Wiley.

PIAGET, J. and INHELDER, B. (1956) *The Child's Conception of Space*. London: Routledge and Kegan Paul.

PIAGET, J. and INHELDER, B. (1969) *The Psychology of the Child*. London: Routledge and Kegan Paul.

PUFALL, P. (1975) 'Egocentrism in spatial thinking'. *Developmental Psychology*, **11**, 297–303.

RICHARDS, M. and BERNAL, J. (1972) 'An observational study of mother–infant interaction'. In BLURTON JONES, N. (Ed.) *Ethological Studies of Child Behaviour*. Cambridge: Cambridge University Press.

ROTHENBERG, B. (1970) 'Children's social sensitivity and the relationship to interpersonal competence, intrapersonal comfort and intellectual level'. *Developmental Psychology*, **2**, 335–350.

RUBIN, K. (1973) 'Egocentrism in childhood: a unitary construct?' *Child Development*, **44**, 102–110.

SELMAN, R. (1970) 'The importance of reciprocal role-taking for the development of conventional moral thought'. Unpublished paper, Graduate School of Education, Harvard University.

SELMAN, R. (1973) 'A structural analysis of the ability to take another's social perspective: stages in the development of role-taking ability'. Paper presented at the meeting of the Society for Research in Child Development, Philadelphia.

SHANTZ, C. (1975) 'The development of social cognition'. In HETHERINGTON, E. (Ed.) *Review of Child Development Research*. **Vol. 5.** Chicago: University of Chicago Press.

STAUB, E. (1971) 'The use of role-playing and induction in children's learning of helping and sharing behaviour'. *Child Development*, **42**, 805–816.

STOTT, D. (1971) *Bristol Social Adjustment Guides Manual*. 4th Edition. London: London University Press.

URBERG, K. and DOCHERTY, E. (1976) 'Development of role-taking skills in young children'. *Developmental Psychology*, **12**, 198–203.

VAN LIESHOUT, C., LECKIE, G. and SMITS-VAN SONSBECK, B. (1973) 'The effect of a social perspective taking training on empathy and role-taking ability of preschool children'. Paper presented at the meeting of the International Society for the Study of Behavioural Development, Ann Arbor, Michigan.

VYGOTSKY, L. S. (1962) *Thought and Language*. Cambridge, Mass: MIT Press.

WEINHEIMER, S. (1972) 'Egocentrism and social influence in children'. *Child Development*, **43**, 567–578.

WENTINK, E., SMITS-VAN SONSBECK, B., LECKIE, G. and SMITS, P. (1975) 'The effect of a social perspective-taking training on role-taking ability and social interaction in preschool and elementary school children'. Paper presented at the Third Biennial Meeting of the International Society for the Study of Behavioural Development, Guildford, England.

WEST, H. (1974) 'Early preschool interaction and role-taking skills: an investigation in Israeli children'. *Child Development*, **45**, 1118–1121.

ZAHN-WAXLER, C., RADKE-YARROW, M. and BRADY-SMITH, J. (1977) 'Perspective taking and prosocial behaviour'. *Developmental Psychology*, **13**, 87–88.

Postscript

The chapters were designed to cover the area. They have *not* been written as a sort of daisy chain wherein each one takes off where the other ends. There are three reasons for this which may become apparent. One is that as research develops in each of the areas studied, an immediate effect is often to alter the point of contact between areas. If you think of a mosaic of evidence, the symptom of a tiny alteration in shape of one element is often first detectable by gaps in its fitting with neighbouring areas. The constant aspect is the centre of gravity of each area, and the shifting one is its liaison with others. If we had dovetailed the chapters too closely it would have become dated prematurely, even if we could have all agreed about the dovetailing.

A second reason is that the source of the work, Piaget's writings, is complex to the point of containing self-contradiction. Some of the contradictions are superficial, some are merely the result of his particular mode of exposition, and some appear to be real points of substance. It requires a high level of talmudic skill to sort out the problems, and we did not wish to tie the book to an exegesis of Piaget. The book represents an evaluation of the work he inspired, not a hermeneutic disquisition on his texts. Therefore, we have avoided the convolutions necessary to harmonize statements with reference to the details of Piaget's own exposition. No orthodoxy has been laid down.

Finally, there are two aspects which form a bundle of disagreement which manifests itself intermittently. Different authors hold differing views on the nature of knowledge and the rules of evidence. I shall give two examples. In chapter 4 of my (1980) book I find myself impelled to study the evidence which Cox deploys in her chapter, and conclude that one of her main lessons is wrong. Which of us is right cannot yet be decided, I am glad to say. Also there I evaluate some infancy work in a way which disagrees with that of Bremner in that I diagnose the limits of the work very differently from him. Again the issue remains open. All that can be said is that on the basis of research results to date, it is possible to pass different judgements on the same body of data according to one's views of where the evidence is heading. At the frontiers of knowledge different people cast their eyes in different directions. But they also come from different places *en route*. Butterworth, for example, begins from a different position on basic epistemological criteria from Bremner. They differ in their views on what kind of knowledge can be extracted from studies of infancy. This can clearly be seen in some of the references to his work listed by Butterworth at the end of his chapter. And it can be immediately seen in this book as Bremner's work takes off from a point in Butterworth's long before the end of Butterworth's chapter. We did not think it profitable to argue out these problems. The chapter-drafts were circulated and no-one felt outraged by any of them. Without censorship one cannot expect to go beyond peaceful coexistence. So we didn't. All that I was asked to do was to write this postscript alerting the reader to what might lie under the surface (if one could agree on the rules of intellectual excavation).

Norman Freeman

Author Index

Numbers in italics refer to pages on which
the complete references are listed.

AUTHOR INDEX

Subject Index